Moving On

Prayer

Jim Graham
PRAYER

Scripture Union
130 City Road, London EC1V 2NJ

Phototypeset by Wyvern Typesetting Limited, Bristol

Printed and bound in Great Britain by
Cox & Wyman Ltd, Reading

Dedication

To my parents
who first taught me how to pray
and to those who have shown me how to continue
especially Anne my faithful prayer partner.

Acknowledgements

To many on whose experience and writing I have drawn.

To Bob Dalton, my Elder, who first of all dissuaded me from writing this book and then felt it right for me to do so and encouraged me in this and in so many other ways . . .

To John Grayston, who spent time with me and gave me so much consideration, for his professional advice and Christian sensitivity . . .

To Pam Kerr who so willingly typed the manuscript and then so painstakingly corrected it with me – and all with such great enthusiasm . . .

. . . I am so deeply grateful.

Contents

1
What is prayer?

There are two kinds of people in the world – those who instinctively respond to circumstances and situations in a *negative* way (for example, 'It is impossible!' 'It can't be done!' 'I will never make it!' 'No one has ever done this before!' 'It is all too big for me – I will have to cut it down to size before I can get involved!') and those who instinctively respond to circumstances and situations in a *positive* way (for example, 'What a wonderful opportunity!' 'There are difficulties – but let's see how they can be overcome!' 'It may not happen *tomorrow*, but I believe it *can* happen!') You will be in one of these two categories. Prayer is normally doomed from the beginning because most of us have not only lost confidence in ourselves, as we see ourselves in the vastness of the universe, but we have lost confidence in God under the influence of materialism and humanism within our society. Yet Christians ought to be the most positive and optimistic of all people, for they know that men and women are unique – they are creatures of two worlds at the same time. They live in the world of space and time and yet they live in an unseen world which breaks in upon their consciousness throughout the day and the night. Sir Thomas

Browne once said that man is 'the great amphibian' – he lives in two worlds at once. That shocking, but intellectually brilliant, Anglican vicar Studdert Kennedy (nicknamed 'Woodbine Willie' by the battered troops of the British forces during World War I to whom he gave 'Woodbine' cigarettes) put this into verse in his own inimitable way:

> I'm a man, and a man's a mixture,
>   Right down from his very birth,
> For part of him comes from heaven,
>   And part of him comes from earth.

Man cannot really be defined or explained in terms of this world alone. Some have tried with ludicrous results. For example, the average man contains enough fat to make seven bars of soap; enough iron to make a medium sized nail; enough sugar to fill a sugar-sifter; enough lime to whitewash a henhouse; enough potassium to explode a toy cannon; enough magnesium for a dose of magnesia; enough phosphorus to make tips for two thousand two hundred matches; and a very little sulphur. All of this could be bought for a few pounds.

This should ensure that one of the dominant features of man is that he is constantly aware that he is living in the realities of another world of unlimited dimensions. This should turn dark pessimism into a balanced and sensible optimism based on a positive Christian hope. Unhappily even the Christian does not often display such an exciting awareness. He, too, lives in a dull, lack-lustre, earthbound existence.

The development of science during this last generation has been astounding. Our children are observing things with a passive nonchalance today which would have been relegated in our childhood to science fiction. Outer space has been pierced; men have landed on the moon; machines have landed on Mars; our world has shrunk until every continent is only a few hours away. There is a cascade of gadgets to make our lives less tedious; anyone who can count to ten can scale mathematical mountains by using a calculator as thin as a credit card and as small as a wristwatch. You can turn a knob or press a button and join an event 10,000 miles away, seeing it with more clarity than those who are there. You can write and be read by thousands. You can speak and be heard by millions.

And yet however amazing the total of man's achievements are we need to write across every one of them – limited!! How sad it is that we settle for the best that the world has to offer (however good and exciting that may well be), and fail to take advantage of the best God has to give! There is a realm that man has been given which has no limit – prayer! It is as limitless as God, for it directly links our life to God. Prayer is limitless in space since it touches three worlds at any given time. It touches heaven, earth and hell simultaneously and instantaneously. It affects God as nothing else will. It touches man at a depth and reality which nothing else can. It disturbs the devil more than any other human enterprise. Prayer is the church's intercontinental ballistic missile in that it travels at the speed of thought; hits the target every time; is fuelled by faith; is fitted with a delayed detonation mechanism; can be directed to any point on earth; and there is no defence against it.

The fact is that man did not think of prayer – God did! This proposition was not agreed by any human conference or committee. God said it and that has settled it for ever! 'Call to me, and I will answer you; I will tell you wonderful and marvellous things that you know nothing about' (Jeremiah 33:3).

We live in a world which has become blasé about enormous resources of natural power. The atomic bomb which fell on Hiroshima in 1945 killed 87,000 people in one second and shattered the lives of countless thousands in the days and months which followed. The hydrogen bomb which was tested in 1952 was a thousand times stronger. With frightening rapidity the American tests on the cobalt bomb in 1954 clearly showed beyond all reasonable doubt that the obliteration of all life on earth was possible. The explosion of a cobalt bomb would produce a radioactive cloud, whose degree of destruction would be three hundred thousand times stronger than the first hydrogen bomb, which in turn, was a thousand times stronger than the first atomic bomb. Mankind now has enough nuclear explosives in the world to eliminate itself many thousands of times over. It is estimated that there is an explosive potential in the world which is equivalent to more than ten tons of TNT for every man, woman and child on the face of the earth. In the light of this, so much of the talk about the escalation of arms in the world is purely academic. Arthur Koestler once said that 'human civilisation is either on the verge of, or in the process of, exploding'. Perhaps, having reached that conclusion, it is not surprising that he and his wife decided to end their own lives rather than to face, as far as they could see, the baleful implications for the future.

How important and exciting it is to affirm with confidence and authority that there is a supernatural power available to the church and the believer in the twentieth century which is virtually untapped. There is a privilege which although recognised, spoken of and discussed widely in Christian circles, is almost wholly neglected . . . prayer! In these days when enormous stockpiles of natural power have become part of our normal life and all over the world the dominating fear and concern is that one day it will be used, and on the other hand severe warnings are being given about the exhaustion of natural energy resources we need to point again to the inexhaustible source of infinite energy open to us through prayer. We need to rejoice that this power is creative and not destructive; positive and not negative; gives birth to hope not despair; is for good and not for evil; and offers life and not death.

Prayer opens the door into dimensions which are beyond our understanding. Prayer is an invitation to experience and explore the boundlessness of God. Many have never really been excited about God, because they have never thought of, far less discovered, his boundlessness. Here he is encouraging us to begin to experience that boundlessness.

Prayer enables us to stand firmly and honestly in the *here* and unquestionably influence the *there*. It enables us, too, to stand in the *now* and effectively touch the *then*. Prayer breaks across the borders of space and the boundaries of time. It cannot be held restrictively in one area or in one era. Millions of prayers have outlasted the nations and dynasties of their contemporaries and arrived safe and sound on the shore of another generation. Who can tell what benefits and blessings others are enjoying in distant lands because we have prayed in this land? Who can tell what mercies and provisions we are now enjoying because we are living in the atmosphere of prayers prayed long ago? No government can cancel the effectiveness of prayer. No law can lock it up within a location or era. No Parliament can kill its influence.

Praying, in one sense, should not be difficult for us – although we are going to see that there are some significant and not inconsiderable obstacles to praying. But prayer is the most natural activity in the world. It really is not an acquired art; it is, rather, an instinct. That great American philosopher, William James, said: 'Many reasons have been given why we should not pray, whilst others are given why we should. But in all this very little is said of the reason why we do pray. The reason why we pray is simply that we cannot help praying.' It is a simple fact gleaned from the anthropologists that no tribe, however primitive and crude its life-style (by our standards in the West), has been found whose people do not pray to such gods as they have. There is something within us which can only be satisfied by crying out to that which is beyond us. Like most of our instincts our 'prayer' instinct needs to be directed and disciplined. Like some of our instincts our 'prayer' instinct can embarrass us and make us awkward when we speak about it. Maybe this is a peculiarly western difficulty since in other lands prayer has become part of the fabric of society. Only last week I spoke with someone who is working on behalf of his company in Saudi Arabia. He clearly found it an inconvenience, if not an irritation, that at regular intervals throughout the working day the board meeting stopped in mid-decision; the planning meeting adjourned; the shutters came down in the shops; the police enforced the closure laws – for prayer!

Yet, in spite of our diffidence in talking about it, far less our reluctance in admitting we are involved in it, our praying is part of our humanity and the divine within us has to appeal to the divine above us. During the last war, when many a bold and arrogant conviction was challenged, a story used to be told of a sergeant who one evening was insisting that he was an uncompromising atheist, and that he had no use whatever for any belief in God. He strongly affirmed that it was weak and childish to subscribe to any form of religious belief – this is a hard world and only hard men make it in the end! The very next day, however, he and some of his men were caught in a dive-bombing raid. As wave after wave of aeroplanes swept down upon their target shattering the earth, exploding human flesh, and blotting out the sun with smoke and acrid fumes, there was nothing else to do but frantically scrabble out a fox-hole in the earth and wait – feeling trapped and petrifyingly exposed. While they waited, as one attack subsided and another could be seen and heard in the distance, in that pathetically shallow shelter the sergeant was busy praying, and unashamedly praying out loud. A soldier waiting there with him said: 'Sergeant, I thought you were an atheist!' 'Son,' said the sergeant, 'there are no atheists in fox-holes.' It needs no argument to prove that in certain circumstances prayer is the universal reaction. In one sense for many of us that is precisely the unconscious error we make about prayer – we tend to connect prayer with the extraordinary and the abnormal – the hour and the moment when life goes disastrously wrong, and we sense that there is nothing that we or anyone else on earth can do about it.

Prayer needs to become a constant part of life – in reality it is an attitude rather than an activity. In the Yorkshire village of Manston, ten miles from Bradford, Smith Wigglesworth was born in 1859 – the year that marked the beginning of the second great evangelical awakening which swept through the United Kingdom and brought a million new Christians into the family of God. The Wigglesworth family were poor and young Smith found himself helping the family income by pulling and cleaning turnips from morning until night – and he was still only six years of age! But the name Smith Wigglesworth became a force to be reckoned with so far as the kingdom of darkness was concerned. God's hand was undoubtedly on him, and even though his methods were somewhat unusual God used him. Throughout the 1920s he travelled extensively; revisiting Australia and New Zealand in 1927; ministering in the heat of Ceylon and India; returning again and again to America and circuiting Europe. His energy for a man turned sixty years of age was amazing; he confounded everyone by ministering three times every day almost everywhere he went. Yet he maintained the touch of God upon his life. In the earlier part of his ministry he used to pray extensively and fast regularly, but in the middle and later years he had learned to 'walk in the Spirit'. He seemed to live in virtually unbroken communion with God. When he was asked if he regularly spent long seasons in prayer, he answered quite unselfconsciously: 'I don't very often spend more than half an hour without praying.'

No doubt such a constant God-consciousness takes time to develop and cultivate – but it is to this way of living that God wants us to turn. The feet need constantly to be firmly planted on earth, yet all the while the head needs to enjoy the revelation and refreshing of heaven. Long ago Jesus said: 'I am telling you the truth: the Son can do nothing on his own; he only does what he sees his Father doing. What the Father does, the Son also does. For the Father loves the Son and shows him all that he himself is doing. He will show him even greater things to do than this, and you will all be amazed' (John 5:19,20).

I think one of the most important lessons that life has taught me is that prayer is not a soft option to facing up to reality. Prayer is never evasion – saving me from having to face things which I do not want to face, and which are going to hurt even if I dare to face them. It was in prayer that Jesus discovered there was no evasion of the cross. It was in prayer that Paul discovered there was no evasion of the person or the people who frustrated, burdened and opposed him in his work. Prayer enables us, not to find a way around the hard thing, but to go straight through it, not to avoid it, but to accept it and overcome it. Prayer is not evasion then; prayer is conquest. Prayer is not an alternative to hard work, careful management, or disciplined living. Prayer does not offer me a way of escape; prayer offers me a way of victory. Jesus did not evade the cross; he went through the cross to the resurrection. Paul did not evade the thorn in the flesh; he discovered that God's power shows up best in weak people, and that there is no limit to the sheer undeserved generosity of God's heart. Thorn or no thorn he saw that God's way was to enable him to be more than a conqueror. So then, I must not pray: 'Lord, take this from me.' Rather I must pray: 'Lord, help me face up to this thing; discover what you are saying and doing in this thing; walk in the power of your Holy Spirit through this thing; and even out of seeming tragedy and darkness find the light of your glory.'

When all is said and done, however, the best definition I know of prayer is that it is **fellowship with God** – sharing my life with God and God sharing his life with me. It is not so much our moving God into our world to solve our problems, as it is God moving us into his world to serve his purposes. I don't understand the rationale of intercessory prayer since I believe God knows and understands the needs of my loved ones and others for whom I pray far better than I do; and I'm sure that he does not need to be reminded of them by me. I can never quite figure out the exact relationship between my prayers of petition and the sovereignty of God. I find it so hard to appreciate that when I make my confession before God on the basis of my repentance he is receiving me as if I were a sinner for the first time, since he doesn't remember that I've sinned before. The older I become the more inadequate I feel my verbal 'thank-yous' are – the deepest gratitudes are really impossible to verbalise. Yet I so often want to breathe out my prayers of thanksgiving to my Father in heaven. I frequently reach out to God and want him to be part of a situation – and yet I know he is not some distant stranger who has to be coaxed and persuaded to get involved; he is 'closer to us than breathing and nearer than hands and feet'. I really don't know how prayer works, and yet I know that God wants me and in my heart I know that I not only need him, but want him too.

There is a lovely story of a little girl who went into church one weekday with her mother. The church was empty, but the mother wanted specially to pray. There was a children's chapel in that church, and while the mother knelt to pray in the main part of the church building, the child went into the children's chapel. The mother had finished her prayers and waited at the church entrance for her little girl to join her. She had to wait for a considerable time. 'What were you doing all this time?' she asked. The little girl said, 'I prayed and said, "Dear Jesus" and he said, "Dear Barbara" and we just loved each other!' This is the essence of prayer, although the story may seem offensive, banal or even puerile to the intellectual and the theologically 'sophisticated'. What would be more natural than in this warm, intimate relationship to share with my Father all that is on my heart – the needs of those who are part of my life; the deepest desires and longings that stir within me; the sense of unworthiness and shame and guilt that would put a gap between him and me; the need to say 'thank you' for so many things; the awareness that I am unable to cope by myself. This is what prayer is!

No one else in the world has permission, nor is in the position, to call God 'daddy' – but the Christian is. The disciples did not ask Jesus to teach them *how* to pray – they knew, because they had been brought up to pray. They were not asking for a *method* or about the *mechanics* of prayer. These men saw and heard Jesus praying and realised there was something fundamentally different – a warm, intimate, moving relationship was being expressed. The unique thing they were

19

witnessing was someone experiencing the fatherhood of God. People who never come to church, who say they believe in God, seldom, if ever, speak of God as *Father*. The reason, of course, is that they are not God's *children*. This makes Christian prayer unique – it is a father/child relationship.

Dr. Campbell Morgan once said, 'Any discussion of prayer which does not issue in the practice of prayer is not only not helpful, but dangerous.' If this book simply tells you what you already know or only informs you of things which you have not really thought about, it has failed! The deepest concern of my heart is that before you go any further you will have the urge to put this book down and enter the adventure of prayer. I would like you to read the four statements I have listed here at the end of this chapter. Read them aloud! Question their truthfulness! I would rather you protest them vigorously than that you agree with them passively. Ask God to confirm them to your heart as you observe your own life and surroundings, and then begin to act accordingly.

1. No Christian's spiritual life will rise to stay above the level of his or her praying.
2. No church's ultimate effectiveness will rise to stay above the level of its corporate prayer life.
3. No church's corporate prayer life will be greater than the personal prayer life of those who make up its membership.
4. No Christian's prayer life will rise to stay above the level of his or her own personal, regular time of worship with God.

2
Hindrances to answered prayer

The twenty-third psalm in the Old Testament is perhaps one of the best known and most deeply loved passages in the Bible. It has captured the joy and hope and confidence of the wedding service and also the desperate loneliness and apprehension and longing of the funeral service. It has verbalised the cry of the human heart in solitude and the confidence in God of the human heart in a vast concourse of people. The previous psalm – Psalm 22 – is not nearly so well-known, and yet it too touches a reality which is firm and familiar.

> My God, my God, why have you abandoned me?
> I have cried desperately for help,
>   but still it does not come.
> During the day I call to you, my God,
>   but you do not answer;
> I call at night,
>   but get no rest.

If our enemy, the devil, cannot keep us from God he will try to bring about conditions in our lives that will hinder God from answering our prayers.

There are some **general** hindrances to prayer itself, but there are also **particular** hindrances to *answered* prayer. We will look at both of these in turn. **Time** is the most devastating hindrance to prayer. Alfred, Lord Tennyson wrote a story many years ago about a king who was dying. The king's servant came to him, and asked, 'Is there something I can do for you?' The old king replied: 'Pray for me, for more things are wrought by prayer than this world dreams of.' Unhappily, while most Christians subscribe to that conviction, few really believe it. We have time for the things which are important to us, and most of us as Christians have concluded that more things are accomplished *without* true prayer than this world dreams of. Our actions contradict our words! Significantly Martin Luther said, 'If I fail to spend two hours in prayer each morning, the devil gets the victory through the day. I have so much business I cannot get on without three hours daily in prayer.' It is said that Charles Simeon devoted the hours of from four to eight in the morning to God. Adoniram Judson suggested, 'Arrange thy affairs, if possible, so that thou canst leisurely devote two or three hours every day, not merely to devotional exercises, but to the very act of secret prayer and communion with God.' I have recalled those whom God has used in his service in a very significant way, not to daunt and discourage, but rather to inspire and challenge to a re-examination of the way that we spend our time.

A few weeks before I was ordained to the Christian ministry and took pastoral responsibility for a church in Dumbarton in the west of Scotland, I went to visit an old minister friend – the Rev. T. A. M'Quiston. So far as I was concerned at that time he had always been old! This meeting took place in his home on the south side of Glasgow not too long before he died. God had used him in a remarkable way over the years. He had a warm, round, animated face with a bristling white moustache. That day he was dressed in a black jacket and waistcoat with black

striped trousers and a white winged collar and wore black boots
– I remember the boots very clearly for no significant reason.
He appeared to me to have remained after the rest of the
Victorians had left Glasgow! With great gentleness and
concern he said to me, 'Mr Graham (he called everyone Mr),
be careful not to have a full diary and an empty heart. You will
constantly be tempted to spend a great deal of time working in
the kingdom, and little time waiting on the King. Make sure
that you don't substitute busyness for blessedness, because
busyness can often lead to barrenness of spirit.' How often his
concern has become meaningful to me over these years. Prayer
has not always been my priority. Many other things – often
most other things – have crowded it out.

Years later a discerning colleague of mine – Len Moules –
had only been part of our pastoral team here for a very few
weeks when he asked how much time I spent in prayer.
Somewhat embarrassed and not a little put out I recognised
that in the pressure of a busy pastorate prayer was not always as
essential as other things. Our priorities are determined by the
way we spend our time (and, incidentally, our money!) much
more than by what we say.

Canon David Watson, whose ministry through preaching,
tapes, and writing has had an incalculable effect and influence,
not only in this nation, but throughout the world, describes a
deeply personal encounter with God many months after his
operation for cancer, but only a few weeks before he died. 'He
showed me that all my preaching, writing and other ministry
was absolutely nothing compared with my love-relationship
with him. In fact sheer busyness had squeezed out the close
intimacy I had known with him during the first few months
after my operation.'

Time is a robber which can plunder the best by
substituting the good. Perhaps, however, alongside time is an
ally in hindering prayer – **indiscipline**. I remember in my
student days hearing someone say that the most important aid
to prayer was a good alarm clock. I am sure that there is a lot of

truth in this, but nevertheless there must always be the discipline of mind over mattress (or whatever else holds us from praying!). Dr Martyn Lloyd-Jones once said that Christianity is far too often presented as a remedy for all our problems: 'Come to the clinic and we will give you all the loving care and attention that you need to help you with your problems.' 'But,' comments Dr Lloyd-Jones, 'in the Bible I find a barracks, not a hospital. It is not a doctor that you need, but a Sergeant-Major. Here we are on the parade-ground slouching about. A doctor is no good; it is discipline we need. We need to listen to the Sergeant-Major – "Yield not to temptation, but yield yourselves to God!" This is the trouble with the Church today: there is too much of the hospital element; they have lost sight of the great battle.' We need to begin now to take stock of the things which we regard as having vital importance and programme these into our way of life. You may well feel that your programme of life creates more difficulties than most, and that if your circumstances were different then it would be much easier. That could be true, but it is more than likely to be an excuse for lack of discipline. I would have thought objectively that being a Christian minister and working every day among Christians in a church building would have made prayer so much easier. There is a public meeting for prayer each morning of the week (except Sunday) in our building. It has been unbelievably difficult to make sure that as far as possible that hour is guarded. There are circumstances which, of course, make it quite impossible, but that would be the unusual rather than the usual. There are five of us on our pastoral team – supported by the church fellowship, and working together daily 'on the patch'. We plan to meet each day at mid-day for prayer – and again it has been such a struggle to hold to that on a regular basis. The big enemy is not circumstances, but **indiscipline**.

Closely allied to **indiscipline** is another general hindrance to praying – our **feelings**. There are the significant times in life when prayer is inevitable and unavoidable. It seems the most natural thing in the world to pray at these times. These occasions, however, are rare. Prayer does not blossom in the area of our feelings, but in the area of our will. In fact most of our Christian life has to be lived in the area of the will and decision rather than the area of the emotions and feelings. Reality cannot be adequately judged on the basis of how I feel about it. It needs to be recognised that the prayer which finds God is one of the most strenuous activities which the spirit of man can undertake. Albert Edward Day, in his book *Existence under God*, describes this true prayer:

It is not merely a flash of Godward desire, but the passionate fervour of the whole self that pants to know God and His will above all other knowing. It is not a hurried visit to the window of a religious drive-in restaurant for a moral sandwich or a cup of spiritual stimulant, but an unhurried communion with God who is never in a hurry. It is not merely the expression of a transient mood of dependence or loneliness, but the consistent cry of one who seeks to perceive and express the ultimate Beauty. It is the antithesis of dilly-dally devotions, drowsy murmurs from a pillow where sleep lies in wait, the lazy lisping of familiar phrases that should shake one to the core of one's being. It is a find-or-die outreach of the soul for God.

Our **view of God** can often be distorted, and this of course will be a major hindrance to praying. All prayer must begin with the conviction that God is more ready to listen to us than we are to speak to him, and even more ready to give than we are to ask. When we pray, we do not go to a grudging, reluctant and unwilling God. Paul writes to the Christians at Rome from the high spirits of his soul, '. . . God, who did not even keep back his own Son, but offered him for us all! He gave us his Son – will he not also freely give us all things?' (Romans 8:32). What more proof would you need – unanswerable proof – of God's open-handed generosity?

There are two prayer parables which Jesus told when he was still on earth; misunderstanding of them has led to a lot of confusion and caused considerable harm. The first of these two parables is the Parable of the Friend at Midnight (Luke 11:5–8). It tells of how a belated visitor arrived at a man's house. It was so late that the man had no food to offer him; and that is a devastating embarrassment in the East where hospitality is a sacred duty. So, although the hour was late, the man went along to his neighbour's home and knocked on his door to get his help in supplying food. The neighbour was in bed and at first refused to respond to the knocking on his door. The embarrassed host, however, continued to knock with shameless persistence. Eventually the man in bed was forced to get up and give him what he needed. The second parable is the Parable of the Unjust Judge (Luke 18:2–8). It tells of a widow who simply wanted justice to be done. In her town there was a judge whose treatment of people and situations was well known for its unfairness – no one ever got a favourable verdict without offering a handsome bribe. The widow could not do this since she had no money. She had tenacity, however, and kept coming back to him until the unjust judge gave her what she wanted because she had worn him down with her persistence.

Often these two stories are taken to mean that if we go on long enough and persistently enough in prayer, we will get what we want. God is represented as one who will respond to our badgering and bombarding him with a barrage of prayer. He is capable of being worn down by our persistence. That is not what Jesus is saying. Persistence indeed is required to demonstrate to God and to ourselves that we are sincere and eager for what we are asking, but that is not the meaning of these two stories. A 'parable' literally means 'something which is laid alongside something else'. It comes from two Greek words *para* which means '*beside*', and *ballein* which means '*to throw*'. When we place two things alongside each other, we do so often for the sake of comparison; but the purpose of the comparison may lie either in *resemblance* or in *contrast*. Many of Jesus' parables do work by resemblance, but the parables of the Friend at Midnight and the Unjust Judge work by contrast. In these parables God is not likened to a churlish and unwilling householder or to an unfair and stubborn judge; he is *contrasted* with such people. What Jesus is really saying is that if a reluctant and churlish householder will in the end give a persistent friend the bread he needs, and if an unjust and insensitive judge will in the end give a widow the justice for which she pleads, *how much more* will God who is a loving father, give us what we need? God is not insensitive and stubborn; nor is he reluctant and churlish – he, in fact, is quite the opposite to these things. He is a loving father who loves to give good gifts to his children, and he neither slumbers nor sleeps.

Once, it is said, a Roman Emperor was celebrating a triumph. He was parading his armies, his captives and his trophies through the streets of Rome. The streets were crowded. At one place on the processional route there was a platform where the Empress was sitting with her children. As the Emperor's chariot passed the place the Emperor's little boy jumped down, dived through the crowd and was about to run on to the road to his father. One of the Roman Legionaries lining the pavement stopped the boy. He swung him up in his arms. 'You can't do that', he said. 'Don't you know who that is? That's the Emperor.' The boy looked at the soldier and laughed. 'He may be your Emperor,' he said, 'but he's my father.' God is undoubtedly God, but God is our *abba* too – our father (in fact our 'daddy' since *abba* is the simplest Jewish word a child will use for its father!).

We need to compare and contrast God with human unwillingness, insensitivity, stubbornness and reluctance. In prayer we are not only coming to our King, but also to our Father. This is what Jesus called God and he taught us to call God that too – especially when we pray! How important for prayer it is to have a right view of God. He is concerned, not only about the *big* things which daunt and defy us, but also about the *small* things which are so important to us and often assume an importance which is quite out of proportion to their significance and value.

Another general hindrance to prayer is **dishonesty**. Martin Luther once said that the first law of prayer is, 'Don't lie to God'. There is a strong tendency when we pray to become conventional and to be very correct in asking for 'right things'. We confuse so often what we want to pray for and what we need to pray for with what we ought to pray for. Sometimes no one would be more shocked than we would be if God in fact gave us what we asked for. We may pray for the giving up of some habit, or for the gaining of some quality or virtue – so that we might be radically and fundamentally changed. All the while we have not the slightest intention of changing, since we are content with things as they are. The rock on which prayer so often founders is pious and meaningless platitudes. To pray without the desire to have God answer is lying to God. If there is something we know we ought to desire, and yet we know perfectly well that we do not really desire it, then our first step must not be to pray for it, but to confess that the holy or the selfless desire which ought to be in our hearts is not there, and to ask God by his Spirit to put it there.

Vagueness in prayer is another frequent hindrance. It is easy to confess before God that we are sinners without ever mentioning the specific sins which make that statement real and personal and significant for us. We can often say to God that we are grateful for all his goodness to us without even beginning to list the multitude of things which have enormously enriched our lives. How natural we find it to ask God to bless us without specifying how we are lacking, and bringing that to God. I often think I can hear God saying to me: 'Son, I know you want me to bless you, but how in particular do you want me to meet your need?' Luke, the writer of one of the Gospels in the New Testament, with his clinical, medical eye, notes that when Jesus was feeding the five thousand he made them 'sit down in groups of about fifty each' so that he could have an accurate estimate of the size of the problem before he 'looked up to heaven'. Four of us from our church were travelling in the Far East, where I had been speaking at a number of conferences. Our final location on that trip had been in the Philippines. In all five countries where we had been, we had always confirmed our onward flight bookings – until we got to the Philippines! Because of our absorption in what we were doing – and also because there was no telephone where we were living – the onward flight booking was not confirmed in advance. It was on the morning of our departure home to the United Kingdom that we decided to make sure all was well – it wasn't! Our seats on the plane to Hong Kong from Manila had gone. The flight to Hong Kong connected with the flight to London – and I really needed to get that specific flight since my father's funeral in Scotland had been arranged for the day after I arrived in London.

When we made the discovery, I can clearly remember that all four of us stood outside the travel agent's office in Manila and asked God's forgiveness for any carelessness or presumption on our part. We asked him to take control of our situation and to get our seats back. The travel agent advised us to go to the airport and deal with the matter. We eventually arrived there, and I confidently believed that all would be well – but, alas, no seats! We considered all kinds of alternatives, but none fitted with my need to be in Scotland the day after the following day. One of our companions reminded me that the previous evening I had been speaking about faith, and how important it was to be specific. We sat down in that crowded, noisy airport in Manila with our air tickets out and specifically mentioned the time of departure and arrival in Hong Kong and the flight number (unforgettably Flight 370, Singapore Airlines). We then had the agonising wait until everyone else had checked in four hours later (a longer four hours I have seldom spent). Nevertheless, we did get on that plane – which was grossly overbooked – and in fact had the best seats of the whole trip of many thousands of miles. The message is now indelibly burned into my spiritual life – BE SPECIFIC!

Assuming these **general** hindrances to prayer have been cleared away, it is good to have a check-list of **particular** hindrances to prayer when positive answers are not being given. Let's be business-like in this prayer business. Here is a good check-list.

1. Unforgiveness
Is there any resentment, criticism, animosity or coldness in my heart towards anyone?

Perhaps there is no more damaging thing to my spiritual life generally and my prayer life particularly than this – Matthew 6:12,14,15; Mark 11:25; Colossians 3:13.

2. Unconfessed sin
Is there anything which I know to be wrong which I am excusing, justifying or unwilling to see as God sees it?

The only way that sin leaves my body is through my mouth as I confess it – Psalm 66:18; Proverbs 28:13; James 4:8.

3. Praying outside the will of God
Can I really ask Jesus to put his signature to my petition to God?

I can pray either selfishly or spiritually – James 4:3; 1 John 5:14; Romans 8:26,27; Hebrews 10:7; John 6:38.

The secret of answered prayer is finding out what God is doing and then joining him – John 5:19.

4. Lack of faith
Do I really believe that God is there although I cannot perceive him with my senses?
Do I really believe that God is personal?
Do I really believe that God is listening and will hear me?
Do I really believe that God will undoubtedly reply?
Do I really believe that God will act?
Do I really believe that God will give me what I ask for? – Mark 11:24; Romans 14:23; Hebrews 11:6; James 1:5–8.

5. Opposition of the enemy
Am I aware that I never pray alone?

When I pray not only do the Father, Son and Holy Spirit join me along with the hosts of heaven, but the hosts of the kingdom of darkness become immediately interested too – Ephesians 4:27; Ephesians 6:11,12 (note that Ephesians 6 is in the context of prayer); James 4:7.

Not only check yourself off against the check-list, but take time to meditate on the passages of the Bible listed under each item on the list – after all, is there a more basic reality in our lives as Christians than having God answer our prayers?

3
Prayer and spiritual warfare

Most of the Christian world seems to have taken a vow of silence on the subject of the devil and spiritual warfare. It is thought generally to be a little extreme, and even fanatical, to give attention to this whole area. It is interesting that the two books in the Bible which have been regarded as most controversial and have received the most destructive attention from some 'scholars' are the book of Genesis and the book of Revelation – the first and the last books of the Bible! Significantly the first exposes Satan's devices and the last emphasises his downfall, destruction and doom. The result is that uncertainty about the devil's existence has been created on the one hand and an air of unreality has been cast over his activity on the other. It is true that he is often blamed for situations where he has not been directly involved – since Christians apparently either dismiss him altogether or allow him to dominate their thinking. However, the devil is a reality even though the world and the flesh also play their part in the confusion and heartbreak which characterise our lives both individually and corporately.

C. S. Lewis in his *Screwtape Letters* makes a very shrewd observation:

There are two equal and opposite errors into which our race can fall about the devils. One is to disbelieve in their existence. The other is to believe, and to feel an excessive and unhealthy interest in them. They themselves are equally pleased by both errors and hail a materialist or a magician with the same delight.

To consign the devil to a malevolent fairyland is just as acceptable to him as an obsessive fanaticism which detects his presence everywhere and in everything. The important thing for us is to recognise that we are dealing with reality here. When the disciples of Jesus asked him to teach them to pray – having seen him at prayer and been captivated by the vibrant reality of his praying – he taught them to pray daily: 'deliver us from the evil one'. Evil is not a force or a concept in the world, but a living being, real and active.

F. C. Vernon-Harcourt assesses the situation with a demanding honesty:

Men don't believe in the devil now, as their fathers used to do,
They have opened the gates of the widest creeds, to let his majesty through.
And never a sign of a cloven hoof, or dart from his fiery bow,
Is seen in all the earth today, for people have voted it so.

But who is mixing the deadly draught, that poisons heart and brain,
And loads the bier of each passing year, with ten hundred thousand slain?
Who blights the bloom of the earth today, with the fiery breath of hell?
If the devil isn't and never was, won't somebody rise and tell?

Who dogs the steps of the toiling saint, digs a pit for his feet,
And sows the tares in the fields of time, wherever God sows wheat?

The sceptic says that the devil's dead, and, of course, what
  he says is true!
But who IS doing the awful work that the devil alone can do?

If there isn't a devil, whence all the sin, and the jarring and
  hideous sounds
That are heard in the senate, the mart and the home, to
  earth's remotest bounds?
It may be true what the scoffer says, that the devil is dead and
  gone
But sensible folks would like to know, WHO CARRIES
  HIS BUSINESS ON?

We need to realise that we are not just called to be God's
sons and God's servants, but we are also called to be God's
soldiers. We need to be constantly reminded that prayer is *to*
God, *through* the Son, *in* the Spirit, *for* man, and *against* the
devil. We must know that any prayer which is to God, through
the Son and in the Spirit is inevitably against the devil. The
devil does not react to people saying their prayers, but he
responds immediately and strongly to those who are really
praying. This '*against*' factor must not be forgotten when we
pray or else we will have a war without an enemy. In Ephesians
6:11–13, the key word in the engagement which we face is
'*against*' –
  . . . stand up against the Devil's evil tricks. For we are not
  fighting against human beings, but against the wicked
  spiritual forces in the heavenly world, the rulers, authorities,
  and cosmic powers of this dark age. So put on God's armour
  now! Then when the evil day comes, you will be able to resist
  the enemy's attacks; and after fighting to the end, you will
  still hold your ground.
In prayer the entrenchments of the enemy must be the primary
target.
  Prayer then is not only worship or work, but warfare. Praise
and thanksgiving enhance worship; intercession and petition

35

influence work; but the word of faith, rehearsing the truth, and resisting the enemy's devices in prayer support warfare. This warfare is no long-distance artillery encounter or opposing the enemy from some far-off missile base, but hand to hand involvement – it is wrestling, according to the Bible. There is something very close, personal, and direct about wrestling! We need, therefore, to be very clear about the character and the characteristics of our opponent.

He is **strong**. This characteristic appealed to that bluff and hearty fisherman, Peter. 'Your enemy, the Devil,' he says, 'roams around like a roaring lion, looking for someone to devour' (1 Peter 5:8). The sheer devastating power of his attack with all its destructive intention is something to be recognised and reckoned with. His strength is enhanced by his **subtlety**. His attacks are not only frontal. The half-truth, the innuendo, the verbalising of what we long to hear about ourselves or others, the element of doubt and uncertainty, our proneness to be beguiled or enticed in some areas of our lives rather than others, are all part of his stock-in-trade. He is a careful planner with thousands of years of experience. He has a cunning and a stealth which lure the unwary. The things he says, the company he keeps, the activities he gets involved in, the Scriptures he quotes, make it all so bewildering and confusing for us – he is wily.

Incredibly, in spite of his aggressive strength, he can be so **sensitive**. He knows where we are most vulnerable at any given time depending on our circumstances. He attacks where we are most likely to give way. It may be in the area of our health, or our marriage, or our children, or our finances, or our future security, or our fellowship with God or with man, or in a dozen other areas. It is not that any of these areas are constant problem areas – but there are times when we struggle in these things, and it is then that he makes his move.

The devil's onslaughts are often **surprise** attacks. He will surprise us in the places he comes to us – it will not always be in the Sohos or Amsterdams of life, but in the Canterbury

Cathedrals or at the Communion Tables of our local churches. He will catch us unawares in that the people he uses are not always the sceptical and the scornful, but those who are avowedly committed Christians and sometimes even those who are joined with us in the local expression of the Body of Christ. He will choose the most unexpected times to move into our lives – it will not always be when we are down and depressed, but often when we have been singularly blessed through some event or circumstance or when in faith we have responded in obedience to the revealed heart of God.

The other characteristic of our enemy is his **speech** – he is the accuser, for that is the meaning of the word 'devil'. He will accuse man to God, but he also accuses God to man. His speech is brilliant, plausible and subtle in its argument. He will take the clear word of God and insinuate that you cannot trust that word – it is insubstantial, invisible, and immaterial. 'Surely,' he taunts, 'you know that God will be unable to help you when your health breaks down or your family life is in confusion or your finances create real anxiety or your job future is uncertain!' This is his oldest strategy of all. As far back as Genesis 3 he came to Eve and spoke into her heart and created doubt about what God had actually said: 'Did God really tell you . . . ?' 'Are you sure that you heard properly when God said . . . ?' Similarly with Jesus his beguiling approach was to cast a shadow of doubt over what God had just affirmed to his Son: 'If you are the Son of God . . .' (Matthew 4:3).

Such are the characteristics of the one who is our adversary, and the church's silence about him and the Christian's disregard of him have simply given him more room to operate unmolested. One of the vital secrets of prayer is to pull down Satan's strongholds. Paul is giving some final instructions to the Christians at Corinth when he says:

It is true that we live in the world, but we do not fight from worldly motives. The weapons we use in our fight are not the world's weapons, but God's powerful weapons, which we use to destroy strongholds. We destroy false arguments: we pull down every proud obstacle that is raised against the knowledge of God; we take every thought captive and make it obey Christ. (2 Corinthians 10:3–5)

As we move positively and directly to 'destroying strongholds' we will be engaging in a form of prayer which accomplishes something which is achieved by no other form of praying or Christian ministry.

We need first of all to define what *strongholds* are (Greek, *ochuroma*). In Greek it is a military word which is synonymous with 'fortress'. It comes from the same linguistic root as the verb which means 'to make firm'. In military language it would refer to an area or a location where the enemy is entrenched. It is precisely the same in spiritual terms. It may be an area of the mind where there is inability to perceive the truth, for Satan's strategy is to blind the mind. It may be an area of the spirit where there is a block and nothing seems able to penetrate. It may be a physical area – because our adversary is concerned to bind bodies. Often it will be largely subconscious, like an iceberg, with only a small portion above the surface.

Any area where Satan has control would come under Paul's description. Sometimes in prayer we shall be moving into enemy territory. We shall see areas of our community, of our national life which have been the domain of Satan yielding to the power of God.

At other times we shall face strongholds of Satan's activity within our own lives. It may be an area of the mind where there is an inability to perceive the truth, for Satan's strategy is to blind the mind. It may be an area of the spirit where there is a block and nothing seems able to penetrate.

I listened to a lady recently who shared how she was unable to love her daughter. Much later, after the whole matter had been dealt with and freedom had come, her daughter said: 'I used to wonder why you always seemed to be angry with me!'

The reason was that that daughter's birth had been after a long, protracted labour. The exhausted mother could think of only one thing – sleep. Her husband – a dear man of God – got into bed and the new baby began to cry. There was another accessible room adjacent, and sensing the need for her husband's presence, that tired mother said: 'Put the baby in that other room.' Her husband refused to do this and spent a long time 'walking the floor' with the new baby in his arms. There came into the mother's mind and settled deep into her subconsciousness: 'He is more concerned for the baby than for me!' Irrational, foolish, untrue though it was – it happened! The enemy built a stronghold there and spoiled a mother-daughter relationship for years. God ultimately showed these two servants of God the reality of the situation – humbling, embarrassing, unspiritual though it was. However, it had to be dealt with – and it was. Freedom came – and so, too, a new relationship between that husband and wife, and that mother and daughter.

Modern psychology seems to have been moderately effective in probing back into one's past to discover the causes of many present problems. It is in the treatment of these problems that success has been less than satisfying. The difficulty is that normally modern psychology would regard man as simply a body and a soul (mind, emotion and will) and disregard that he is also spirit. So a whole dimension of our being is obscured from treatment. There are physical and 'soul' problems which will disappear only when a spiritual dimension is recognised and dealt with.

The existence, however, of a problem does not mean that the devil has a stronghold in our lives. For instance, the existence of worry does not mean that a person has a stronghold of worry. The probability is good, however, that if one gives in to worry much and often, there will soon be a stronghold in which that person is held captive and the matter of worry is no longer voluntary, but compulsive.

In summary, a stronghold may be defined as a system of

thought or an area of bondage within the body or soul which encourages the devil. The full treatment of this subject would require a volume on its own. Our concern here, however, is to deal with **prayer** and **strongholds**.

Having *defined* a stronghold, how do you *detect* it? Compulsions, fixations, obsessions, involuntary thought processes which constantly recur must certainly be included as suspects for strongholds. Unreasoning fear, helpless hate, insurmountable jealousy, uncontrollable temper, or a ruthless, aggressive spirit may well be symptoms of a stronghold. Tell-tale signs often are constantly demanding lust, unchecked appetites and undeniable urges. Lack of self-restraint, impatience, and even indecision can be signs of a developing stronghold.

Over the years in the pastorate – and certainly of more recent years – I have counselled people who were struggling with what I believed were strongholds of rejection (this is such a common problem!), lust, timidity, distrust, criticism and a variety of phobias. No amount of encouragement or enlightenment over the problem would help. But when the matter was diagnosed as a stronghold of a spiritual nature and was dealt with on that basis – often healing would come. How much we are dependent on God to help us be relevant as well as real in these matters. How humbling it is to realise that experience, training and ability contribute comparatively little, only God can do it, and bring glorious freedom.

Having *defined* and *detected* a stronghold we are then in a position to move in to *demolish* it! We are encouraged in the Bible to recognise that our weapons are strong and effective. However, it is not specified in the Bible what our weapons are. We are reminded that our weapons are not those which men can provide, but those which God alone can provide.

The Word of God seems to be chief among our weapons. It is described as the 'sword of the Spirit' in the list of items of spiritual armour (Ephesians 6). So it is not *our* sword, but *his*. The 'belt of truth' seems to encompass the Bible, whereas the sword of the Spirit is pulled out from the belt of truth and is the relevant word from God to meet that particular and specific need.

The name of Jesus and the blood of Jesus are powerful weapons in spiritual warfare. The all-conquering name of Jesus includes all that he IS – and after all he is within us in all the power of his risen life by his Spirit if we have been born again; and the One who is within us is greater than the one who is in the world. His blood stands for all that he DID on our behalf at Calvary and embraces the victory he won over the enemy there. 'Our brothers won the victory over him,' cries John in the last book of the Bible, 'by the blood of the Lamb and by the truth which they proclaimed; and they were willing to give up their lives and die.' The blood of Jesus, coupled with Christian testimony and total commitment, will undoubtedly mean the undoing of the devil.

The armour of God in its totality (Ephesians 6) and the power of the Holy Spirit are also part of the arsenal of our spiritual weaponry. Our concern here, however, is to know what to do to assault the strongholds of Satan and demolish them. We have a clear assurance from the Bible that our spiritual weapons will accomplish four things:

1. Destroy strongholds.
2. Destroy false arguments – and this not by intellectual expertise or logical prowess, but supernaturally. How offensive this is to many!
3. Pull down every proud obstacle that is raised against the knowledge of God – is this our traditions, our culture, our customs, our prejudices? Perhaps there are so many more 'proud obstacles' which obscure the light of God and defy the life of God permeating our lives.
4. Take every thought captive and make it obey God. It is an unbelievable thing that through our praying even thoughts are made captives – you and I can have an effect on the thinking of those around us.

In practice, how do we set about waging such spiritual

warfare? It will certainly be on our knees before God in total dependence upon him! Let me give you some clear guidelines:

1. Begin with yourself.
2. Identify the stronghold.
3. Confess the sins that have helped that stronghold to be built and may even have caused it.
4. Dismiss the enemy, even as formerly you have encouraged him.
5. Declare that you are God's property and that he (the devil) is a trespasser.
6. Confess that your body is the house of the Holy Spirit who lives within you.
7. Take your stand against any encroachment of the enemy in your mind, emotion and will as well as your body.
8. Declare your right to be free in Jesus Christ and receive that freedom consciously.
9. Thank God with all your being for what he has done for you.
10. Be ready to help others become whole people in Jesus.

4
Praying in the Spirit

Lehmann Strauss in *Sense and Nonsense about Prayer* says:

If anyone were to ask me what is the first truly great secret of a successful prayer life, I would say in answer, 'Praying in the Holy Spirit'.

When the Christian begins to pray there is tremendous help and encouragement for him. He has permission and is in the position of speaking to God as his Father. Those who are not Christians will seldom, if ever, speak of God as 'my Father'. They do not because they cannot. But Jesus encouraged Christians to do just that. We are so often overwhelmed by the problems of prayer that we allow the enormous privilege of prayer to escape us. Some weeks ago I was invited to have lunch in London with an old friend from the United States. It was an outstanding lunch, and we had a magnificent view into the gardens of Buckingham Palace. Afterwards I went to his hotel room to continue our conversation. He was obviously eager to share that only a few weeks previously he had had an audience (if that is the right way to describe it!) with the President of the United States of America, Ronald Reagan. He told in graphic detail all that had happened and recalled the conversation which had taken place. He also had a photograph of the President shaking his hand! Apparently they over-ran the allotted time by a few seconds – the allotted time was ten minutes! Memorable! Thrilling! Prestigious! – and all that with a man who one day will pass from the face of the earth and have his name recorded briefly in the unfolding history of the human race. I would not want to take anything away from the drama and privilege of that event – but in prayer we have the opportunity of having an audience with the eternal God of the universe. He never closes his office or switches on the Ansafone. He never goes off duty or falls asleep on duty. God, our Father, is listening to his children whenever they make contact with him.

So far as God the Son is concerned he is constantly interceding (putting our case) before his Father and ours on our behalf. Jesus is not only on God's side, he is on ours too. We have often so stressed the divinity of Jesus that we have neglected his present humanity. Jesus' work did not end on the cross – he eventually ascended to his Father to plead with him on our behalf among other things. I have never been able to discover why the Ascension of Jesus was neglected in my early years, although I went to church regularly. Maybe it was because our church was so anti-establishment or maybe because Ascension Day always fell on a Thursday – and nothing ever happened in our church on a Thursday! As a result the Ascension never received the attention from the pulpit that Easter did, or even Christmas. Whatever the reason, it was a great spiritual impoverishment. I cannot remember anyone ever telling me that I was continually on Jesus' prayer list – even if everyone else forgot all about me, he never did! It really is so comforting, and brings so much security to know that there is a Man in heaven even now, as I write and as you read, who knows all about the tensions and temptations, the laughter and the tears, the delights and the disappointments of life here on earth, and he is praying for us.

As if all that were not enough, God the Holy Spirit is also

involved when we come to prayer. With what I sense is breathless wonder that human dynamo Paul writes to the Christians at Rome and says:

> . . . the Spirit also comes to help us, weak as we are. For we do not know how we ought to pray; the Spirit himself pleads with God for us in groans that words cannot express. (Romans 8:26)

The word in Greek for 'helps' literally means 'to lay hold along with, to take hold with another'. The implication is that prayer is a double harness, a dual responsibility. God brings about the need in our lives and we decide to pray. When we do, the Spirit 'helps' us.

The Bible never deludes us that a consistent prayer life is easy or natural. But it does comfort us with the assurance that there is One who comes to our rescue as we struggle – the Holy Spirit. This is his remarkable job – to help us in our greatest needs. Often prayer is one of our greatest needs. Not only, then, do I have Someone speaking on my behalf in heaven, but there is Someone else on earth stimulating reality and helping me with my difficulties in prayer – the Holy Spirit.

When there are things on my heart that I find so difficult to put into words with my lips – he helps me. When there are words on my lips that are not really expressing honestly what is on my heart – he helps me. Some months ago I was speaking at a conference in Indonesia at which 98% of those present were Indonesians who did not speak English. I knew what I wanted to say, but no matter how I said it, they would never understand and it would be a waste of their time and mine. I was given an interpreter, Ronnie Sigarlaki, a delightful Indonesian lawyer, to meet this need. I told him what I wanted to say and he said it in a way that the whole Conference understood. I was told by someone who was fluent in both Indonesian and English that he said it better than I told him. Undoubtedly that was why it was such a memorable Conference week! In a comparable way the Holy Spirit is our Divine Interpreter. He says, in effect: 'You tell me what you want to say, and I will say it for you; you tell me your difficulties and I will help you.'

Notice carefully that he will not pray *for* us, but he will pray *with* us. He requires our *co-operation*. He is looking, not for our *passive* submission, but for our *active* submission. How does 'praying in the Spirit' work then?

He is prepared to help us in two areas – and both are important. One area is our **experience** of prayer, whilst the other is our **expression** of our prayers. He wants us to allow him significantly and overtly to influence our experience of prayer, and also to allow him to influence our expression of prayer. It really is up to us whether we allow him to have his way in both these areas or not. He will not force us – but he longs to co-operate with us, and for us to co-operate with him. In both areas our active participation is required.

Let us, first of all, see how he wants to influence our **experience** of prayer. For example, in the area of our *feeling*; our *desiring*; our *wanting*; we often have major problems in prayer. I have discovered both personally, and through the comments of others, that our real problem in prayerlessness is seldom lack of time or lack of energy, but lack of wanting. There is always both time and energy for the things that are top priorities for us and important to us. I clearly remember I was under a lot of pressure getting prepared to get off to a Conference to speak. I had got up very early on the morning of departure, and I was really struggling to leave things in order before going off. Then my son appeared on the doorstep obviously injured and in great pain. He had been playing football and had crashed heavily with an opponent.

At that moment nothing mattered to me but that. Making sure all was well at the home church where I was a pastor; ensuring that I had all I needed to be relevant at the Conference; getting to the Conference on time – important as those things were, my son's injury and pain were much more important to me. So the next hours were spent in taking him to the hospital; having him X-rayed; having the injury diagnosed as a broken collar bone; getting his arm bound up properly to allow proper healing to take place – then, and only then was I free to continue what I had been doing. We often suffer from the 'malady of not wanting' in our praying. Why not be honest and say so – because prayer has become dull, mechanical, routine, lack-lustre. Why not say: 'God, I am in difficulties here, would you please help me as you promised.' There is an enthusiasm and a euphoria in prayer that can be created within our flesh, but it is superficial and does not satisfy anyone – not even ourselves. Ask the Holy Spirit to give that deep yearning, real longing and reaching out with a passionate heart after God in prayer – and he will! This is praying 'in the Spirit'.

Again, in the area of our *mind* we struggle so much. We lack the ability to know what we ought to be praying for and the knowledge of how to do it even when we do know. That is often compounded by wandering thoughts and inability to concentrate. It all leads to an unreality and dissatisfaction. Pretence and deadness in prayer quickly follow. Why not ask the Holy Spirit to help you here? The word 'wisdom', when it is used in the Bible, means 'the ability to see things from God's point of view'. How I need to be able to do this, and how the Holy Spirit longs to help me. He wants to put his impressions, his ideas, his thoughts, his vision, his burdens into my mind so that I would consciously know what to pray for. He wants to lead and instruct me like a little child how to pray for that which he has put into my mind if I will only take time and give him the opportunity to do so. He wants to take the natural, and inevitable, wandering thoughts and lack of concentration and gently and supernaturally captivate my mind with the glory and goodness of God. This is 'praying in the Spirit'.

Yet again, in the area of my *will* – I often know what I want to do, and sometimes even long to do it. No matter how often I am stimulated to pray realistically, and no matter how often I determine to ensure that it happens – after a few days it breaks down yet again. A sense of guilt, failure and even disillusionment can so often be the accompaniment of this breakdown. Is there no help for me? Yes there is! The Holy Spirit wants to heal, strengthen and give a cutting edge to my will so that there will be a new persistence in what I have set myself to do. There is nothing in me that can achieve or maintain this – but the Holy Spirit can and will! This is 'praying in the Spirit'.

The Holy Spirit wants to take the mind and will of God and impart it to us. Listen again to Paul's thrilling assurances:

> And God, who sees into our hearts, knows what the thought of the Spirit is; because the Spirit pleads with God on behalf of his people and in accordance with his will (Romans 8:27).

This is praying in the Spirit – having confessed my sin and received the cleansing of God; having reached out in faith believing that God is, and that he hears, listens and will reply to me; knowing that he can change things as well as people; assured that he wants me to know what he wants; I can trust the Spirit's ministry to me. So I can begin to pray the will of God into my own life, and into the lives of others. When the Holy Spirit is helping your thoughts in prayer you will have the will of God your Father in your prayers. This is the joy of praying in the Spirit.

The Spirit's ministry is to bring glory to our Lord Jesus Christ. This is why he came! He is not in conflict or competition with Jesus, but wants to confirm who he is and what he does. To 'pray in the Spirit' will inevitably lead to honouring and exalting our Lord Jesus. So much of our praying exalts us, or our programme, or our projects, or our church, or our Christian enterprise, and it is all so man-centred – praying 'in the Spirit' will leave the glory with none but Jesus. This will so clearly characterise 'praying in the Spirit'.

Another clear mark of 'praying in the Spirit' is that our prayers will always have echoes, and the content, of the Word of God. God never contradicts his Son, nor does he ever speak contrary to his Word. After all, the Spirit was the One who imparted the Word of God to those who wrote it down in the Scriptures. It is not that necessarily we will quote Scripture from one of the many translations, but biblical principles and precepts will never be dismissed nor denied when we are 'praying in the Spirit'. On the contrary we shall welcome them and delight in them.

So one of the main evidences of 'praying in the Spirit' is when we are open, listening, submissive, and responsive to the influence of the Spirit when we are in the **experience** of prayer. Our thoughts, attitudes, and desires are under his control although clearly expressed by us.

We need to turn now to the other main evidence of 'praying in the Spirit', where we allow him to control our **expression** in prayer. Again he wants our co-operation as we use the means God has given us to express anything – our lips and tongue. This form of 'praying in the Spirit' is unknown to some Christians today, but is becoming familiar and natural to an increasing number. Here our minds are not involved. Instead of actively forming our own words in the mind we allow the Holy Spirit to control us. He directs our prayer at the deeper spiritual level of our beings and what he stimulates there we express verbally through our mouths.

There are a number of evidences of this in the Bible. It can sound sometimes like *groaning*. Again let us return to Paul's encouraging words: '. . . the Spirit also comes to help us, weak as we are. For we do not know how we ought to pray; the Spirit himself pleads with God for us in groans that words cannot express.' Often throughout the history of his people Israel God listened to and responded to their groans. Is it not so that sometimes we have longings which are so deep; burdens that are so heavy and bewildering; and passions and yearnings within us which are so intense that interpreting them into words and then verbalising how we are is beyond us? So it is with the Spirit as he helps us in our praying before God.

Sighing is another expression which bypasses the mind.

49

Deep within us is inexpressible longing. In the history of the Hebrews God listened to the sighing of his people on several occasions. Haven't we so limited and restricted prayer by confining it rigorously to words being expressed?

Yet another of the expressions of the Spirit's ministry within us and from us is *crying*, not hysteria or emotionalism or sentimentality, but a quiet, gentle weeping before the Lord. Sometimes it will be when we are quite overwhelmed by the Lord's presence or filled with adoring wonder at the evidence of his power at work before us. Sometimes it will be when we reach out with a compassion beyond our ability to rationalise when we realise the desolating poverty of a situation or the incalculable pain caused by someone's circumstances – this is 'praying in the Spirit'.

Perhaps, however, the most difficult area of all for many in 'praying in the Spirit' is when the Spirit wants to make us fluent in a language which we do not know and we have never learned. It is so sad that the language which the Spirit gives to the godly heart is so glibly and unhelpfully dismissed as 'tongues'. That hardly describes the ultimate fluency which the Spirit will give as we actively submit to him and co-operate with him. 'Tongues' can so easily convey the idea of babbling hysteria or ecstatic speech. It is neither! There is nothing to be feared surely in a language which has syntax and grammar – even if we do not understand it, or even if it is a language of heaven.

The disciples of Jesus had been gathering for prayer for ten consecutive days when the Holy Spirit came upon them on the day of Pentecost. Rather than using their normal thought patterns God released them spontaneously and supernaturally in praise in such a way that the community was arrested by the reality. So his Holy Spirit was displayed in a unique way.

Over the years I have read a number of books on the life of the Apostle Paul. Most of them have been helpful, but none that I recall – even those which have given attention to Paul's prayer life – have taken into account his statements about, and his personal experience of, praying in the Spirit. 'I would like all of you to speak in strange languages,' he declared to the Corinthian Christians (1 Corinthians 14:5). 'I thank God that I speak in strange languages more than any of you,' (1 Corinthians 14:18) he testified to that divided, difficult church at Corinth which apparently was well versed in the reality and functioning of the gifts of the Holy Spirit.

As I look at the confusion, abuses, fear and divisiveness that the gifts of the Holy Spirit (especially the gift of languages) have caused, I can only conclude that an enemy has caused this. You see, when we pray in this way the devil knows well that a new freedom, joy and significance is breaking in on the prayer life of God's people. He knows, too, that every word of that prayer is exactly right. His usual stock-in-trade is to drive human beings to an extreme position. That he has done well – and so far as the gift of languages is concerned he has made some quite fanatical over this gift, whilst many, many others have become quite fearful.

To those who would decry and despise the Holy Spirit's gift of speaking in a 'prayer' language I would want to remind them that this was the first gift that God gave to his church on its birthday. To those who would protest its irrelevance as being the lowest of the gifts of the Holy Spirit I would counsel that that is a really good place for all of us to begin. To those who fear abuse or counterfeit, I would want to plead that an abuse is not dealt with by non-use, but by right use and a counterfeit presupposes a reality.

Normally this **expression** of prayer is for private use – often for worship and sometimes for intercession. Many of us have been left speechless as we come to worship God and catch a glimpse of his glory, his goodness and his grace. How good of God to help us here to express the inexpressible – what release! what joy! what wonder! Emotion? Indeed, but reality! Most of us have been in the situation of praying for someone or something when we frankly had no idea how we ought to pray. What a privilege to lift that up before the Lord in the perfect language of the Holy Spirit!

Where the Spirit's language is used in public then there are clear biblical guidelines laid down. It must, for example, always be interpreted so that understanding, as well as utterance, is present. Only two or three will be allowed to use their language and only one at a time. There will be no incoherent babbling which is so disconcerting and difficult for the 'outsider' to handle. The interpretation – even in public – will normally be addressed to God and not man. Occasionally the Spirit's language with an interpretation (note: not a translation) will equal a prophetic word to the congregation. But God is a God of order, and freedom in the Spirit is not an opportunity nor an encouragement to depart from that. One of the flavours of the fruit of the Spirit is self-control. Uncontrolled behaviour in public – or indeed in private – is not evidence of the Spirit, but normally shows the flesh at work, and occasionally the devil at work. You may well ask: '*Must* I pray in this way?' No, there is no compulsion – but that is the wrong question. The right question is: '*May* I pray in this way?' Yes, you may! Ask the Lord Jesus to enable you to pray in this way and then co-operate with the Holy Spirit in doing so.

I had been invited to speak at the Strathpeffer Convention in Scotland some years ago. I travelled north on the overnight train from London. I eventually arrived in Inverness a bit travel-weary. Having had breakfast, I took a coach through some breathtakingly beautiful countryside to Strathpeffer. My hosts were so kind and hospitable, and my first meeting with the Council of the Convention was at lunch. Around the table the conversation turned to some of the outstanding Conventions of the past with many names being mentioned which I had regarded throughout my youth and young manhood as spiritual giants. I felt dismayed and uncomfortable and completely out of my depth. I quickly doubted the wisdom (or was it the pride?) which had encouraged me to accept the invitation to speak at the Convention. The sermons which I had carefully and prayerfully prepared seemed to be wrong – unsuitable and inadequate. I withdrew into silence as the conversation continued and felt a deep longing to go home. The days that stretched ahead filled me with a great foreboding. The Convention did not begin until the evening of that day and some of the Council members were so warmly inviting their guests to go for a drive in the beautiful Scottish Highlands. I declined on the grounds of tiredness – which was perfectly true. I returned to my hotel bedroom and in despair knelt down. I read two or three Psalms and as I knelt there beside the bed I lifted my heart in desperation to the Lord – and found myself pouring out my soul in a language I had never learned. I had been baptised in the Holy Spirit about two years previously – but oh the release, the wonder, the freedom of that afternoon when I got before the Lord with a full stomach, but with an empty, aching heart!

Before you continue reading this book there are some questions which require answers:

1. In the light of the biblical teaching how would you define and describe praying in the Spirit?
2. Will you consciously submit your feelings, mind and will to the Holy Spirit now?
3. Will you consciously submit your lips to the Holy Spirit in an act of co-operation as you would worship God and intercede for others in order that you might receive his gift to help you in prayer in whatever way he chooses?

5
Praying for others

Only last evening one of the members of our church stood up, unannounced and unasked, in the church to say thank you for our prayers for her and her mother over the past few months. Her mother, suffering from a terminal illness and given only two weeks to live, was again about the house, dressed and taking her responsibility with the household chores. It was so simple, straightforward and unexpected that it brought tremendous refreshing and joy to us all. There was something about it which was so natural and unspectacular – her name and her mother's name had appeared on our weekly church bulletin, and the fellowship had been encouraged to pray. We did.

I know that these things happen all over this land and other lands – and yet we struggle so much to get going and then to believe that it is worthwhile and effective to pray for others.

One of my old teachers who gave me a love for the New Testament, and so much encouragement to be involved in the ministry of the church, Dr William Barclay, says:

In intercession we take the needs of the world and bring

them to God for His blessing and His help. We remember before God those in illness and distress of mind and all those whom we know specially to need God's blessing.

Intercession is simply praying for others. I have really struggled in my mind over the years about the validity of praying for others. Surely God knows their needs far better than I ever could? Surely my heavenly Father wants to meet those needs without my asking him to do so? In any case, since he is God eternal presumably he doesn't need to be reminded by me of the situations and circumstances of people! One of the enormously strengthening and stabilising realities of my life is the awareness of the sovereignty of God – but I find it so difficult to work out the actual connection between my asking and his sovereignty. Yet I know that unquestionably God wants us to pray for others – and it works!

One of the characteristics of the people of God is that they 'will be known as the priests of God' (Isaiah 61:6). I know that this is one of the highest privileges of all of us who are in God's family, and yet not everyone exercises it. I made some brief notes in my notebook about what a priest did. Here are my findings:

1. His work

The priest lives with God and for God (Deuteronomy 10:8) and he lives with man and for man (Hebrews 5:1). In other words he is on God's side as well as on man's side.

So the priest operates on two dimensions at the same time – the divine and the human.

This surely is prayer!

2. His walk

God is more concerned about what a man is than about what he does.

His clothes are important (Exodus 28). Presumably this is

because the outward often (though not always) speaks clearly of the inward condition and desire of his heart.

His relationships and contacts are to be pure so that he will be undefiled (Leviticus 21).

The blood of sacrifice and oil are to be imprinted on him – a reminder of his need for *pardon* so that there will be no hindrance before God; and *power* so that there will be effectiveness before God.

What a pity the doctrine of the priesthood of all believers has been prostituted to shore up the political and non-biblical practice of democracy within the church. The profound truth is that it is an affirmation by God that all of us can come right into his presence to present our own needs and the needs of others before him without any reservation.

It is easier to pray for ourselves, however, than to pray for others, and yet the difficulty must never prevent the reality occurring.

Why do we pray for others?

Some have never really begun seriously to do this, whilst others do it without thinking honestly about why they do so. The human heart and mind are skilled in the art of deception – especially self-deception. We do not mean it to be, but unconsciously it is. Prayer is not manipulation – it is not white magic! Prayer is not me getting God to do what I want. Nor is prayer God getting me to do what he wants. Prayer is me getting God to do what he wants. All that is honest within us cries out that that will happen anyway since God is God. Apparently this is not so – and our prayers are effective not only in changing people, but also in changing situations.

Prayer does not infringe people's freedom – for God never does that – but it does reinforce what God is already accomplishing within that situation about which we are praying. There are really only two reasons why we should pray for others, and we need to state these in the form of questions. First of all, if my prayer for this person or that situation were answered *would the glory of God be seen?*

That word 'glory' can be used glibly. What do we mean? Glory has two ideas contained in it. One is the idea of heaviness, or weight, or worthiness or fullness. The other is the idea of brightness without shadow or distortion. When prayer for others is answered then the question that must be constantly in our minds is 'will people be left in no doubt that this is God, for God's nature is clearly seen in it? Will they recognise that only God could have accomplished what has happened?'

Secondly, if my prayer is answered will it really be *for the good of the person for whom I am praying?* It is so easy to allow both self-interest and/or self-righteousness to influence and even dominate my praying for others. For example, in praying for someone very close to us – a husband, a wife, a parent, a child – to become a Christian it is so easy to allow self-interest to motivate us. We can pray for their conversion because we know that that would make life easier, smoother, more comfortable, and happier for *us*. In praying for someone like that it is normally much more helpful to concentrate on thanking God for the many qualities that they display which are good and honourable and admirable, and at the same time to pray for yourself that God will make you a better husband, wife, parent or child. That is often a much more effective way to pray in such a situation and more likely to accomplish what God is longing for. It will certainly eliminate any possiblity of praying for our own benefit. Again, self-righteousness can so spoil our praying for other people. It is so easy in public intercession to pray *at* others rather than to pray *for* them – to turn praying into a form of preaching. I have occasionally seen a prayer meeting in our own church ruined by one, or maybe two, people fervently 'praying' by implication: 'you are not praying for the things you *ought* to be praying for – the things that I am involved in, and *you* ought to be involved in them too!' It is so easy in private intercession to pray: 'Lord, make everyone in the church as willing, thoughtful, selfless and keen as I am!' In private it is sad; in public it is disastrous; and I cannot believe that God wants to or will answer any such praying.

How can I ensure that my motives in praying for others are pure and honouring to God? By asking what you would be willing to lose in order for that prayer to be answered. By asking how many people you pray for from whom you can receive no benefit whatsoever. During my first months in the ministry after my ordination I was invited to share in a prayer meeting each Monday morning with the local Congregational minister and the local Free Church of Scotland minister. The prayer meeting took place in the vestry of the Free Church of Scotland in Dumbarton. The Free Church minister knelt – and I found that difficult since I was accustomed when praying to crouch with my face in my hands or sometimes to sit upright with my eyes closed, my legs crossed and my arms folded. His posture didn't really disturb me – for after all he came from a different church tradition from me – but the intensity and language of his prayer sometimes did. Occasionally he would pray that God would make us willing to become the 'off-scouring of the earth like the Apostle Paul' in order that men might be saved. I did not know my Bible well enough to fit that phrase into its context. I now know the context and it disturbs me still. Paul is writing to the Christians in Rome and sharing with them the concern he has for his own people the Jews – many of whom lived there, '. . . for my people, my own flesh and blood!' he says. 'For their sake, I could wish that I myself were under God's curse and separated from Christ.' I still struggle personally with going that far in praying for others – for that surely is the ultimate in selfless intercession. I realise that Moses, too, in the Old Testament had a similar depth of selfless concern for his own people – that God would blot Moses' name out of his book if he wanted, in order that his people might be safe. The point to which I am prepared to go is not the major issue, but the question needs to be asked: 'In praying for others what would I be willing to lose in order that my prayer might be answered?' This is the right attitude which will ensure that neither self-righteousness nor self-interest is motivating my praying for others.

Who should we be praying for?

In praying for others this is the second question we need to ask. It would be good to take time to make a list of categories – and then fit names into them. My list of categories extends to four – and all of these have a clear biblical warrant.

First of all the Bible instructs us to pray for the *sick*. There are a number of activities connected with the sick that we are encouraged to adopt. The sick, for example, are instructed to call for the elders of the church who will anoint them with oil, and pray for them (James 5:14–16). Again, believers are encouraged to 'place their hands on sick people' and they will get well (Mark 16:18). It would seem, too, that physical and emotional illness would come into the category of a 'hill' or a 'mountain' which needs to be removed – and to that a clear, authoritative word without doubt can be spoken and a positive result secured (Mark 11:23). There is a curious reference in the captivating unfolding of the church's exploits during the first generation after her birth regarding Paul's ministry. The 'handkerchiefs and aprons he had used' were taken to the sick and those in demonic bondage and healing and freedom resulted (Acts 19:11,12). The 'power to heal' is listed as one of the gifts of the Holy Spirit to demonstrate the conduct of Christ (1 Corinthians 12:9). But through all of these there rings a promise of Jesus which surely has relevance when confronted with sickness: 'For this reason I tell you: when you pray and ask for something, believe that you have received it, and you will be given whatever you ask for' (Mark 11:24). Whatever the sick person does, and whatever others may do for the sick person, I need to pray for that person from my heart.

We have good biblical instruction, too, to pray for *the servants of the Lord*. As far as I can see, our first concern for the Lord's servants is neither their safety nor their comfort, but rather that they will be bold in witness and ministry, and that God will open up ways whereby his Word would have the opportunity to enter in the power of the Holy Spirit. It is not wrong to pray both for their safety and their comfort, but these are not the first considerations! It is always a lurking danger that we are more concerned about man's wants than God's desires. In the same context we are to pray that God will send out people to gather in a rich harvest. With his heart deeply stirred with compassion Jesus said: '. . . the harvest is large, but there are few workers to gather it in. Pray to the owner of the harvest that he will send out workers to gather in his harvest.' There are over 2,700,000,000 people today who have never heard the gospel at all, and there are only between 5,000 and 7,000 missionaries worldwide working directly with these totally unreached groups of people. That means there is approximately *one* missionary for every 450,000 people – hardly over-staffing! It is estimated that 80,000 unsaved people die every day (approximately 3,333 every hour or 55 people every single minute of every day). We need to hear the disturbing logic of Oswald J. Smith again: 'No one has the right to hear the gospel twice, while there remains someone who has not heard it once.' The adult population of England and Wales is approximately thirty-nine million. Of these about four million are linked with a local church and attend public worship on average at least once a month. That leaves thirty-five million who are not linked with a church – these are the unchurched of our day. That will include those who have a religious faith, though not a Christian one, for example Muslims, Buddhists, Sikhs or Hindus, etc. Prayer is God's answer to this need. It may mean, of course, being led by the Spirit to go to someone, as God has revealed it to you, and saying: 'Could it be that God is laying his hand upon you for special assignment at home or abroad?' Even more personally, it will be that sometimes God will say to you, if you dare 'pray to the owner of the harvest that he will send out workers', with alarming clarity, 'I want you to be part of the answer to your prayer'.

Praying for the Lord's servants is a dramatic activity and sometimes it can become awesomely personal.

Perhaps not such a well-known category in which we are instructed to pray for others, is to pray for our *politicians*. They have plenty of publicity, but they are woefully short on prayer. I do not mean that we should give them a passing reference by name from time to time – but that we should learn about their personal situation and be informed about their political and practical stand on issues which concern our society. Out of knowledge we should pray for them. R dicule, satire, caricature, and criticism are all directed against them – isn't it time we really prayed for them?

As well as our own Member of Parliament, Senator or whatever, we need to remember those who have responsibility for maintaining law and order – the Lord Chief Justice, the Attorney General, the Master of the Rolls or their equivalents. It would seem that the gospel historically needs certain political conditions to enable it to be preached, heard and responded to. It is for this reason that political stability and social law and order need to be secured. Those in authority have a responsibility to do just that. In this regard, isn't it curious that the church in China has made a far more significant impact and has grown numerically at an astonishing rate under Communism than under Capitalism? Certain conclusions may well be drawn from this. Thought certainly needs to be given to it.

The fourth category that the Bible enjoins us to pray for is our *enemies*. It is relevant to ask: 'How many people do I regularly pray for who oppose me, make life difficult for me, clearly do not like me?' The best way, of course, to dispose of your enemy is to make him your friend. And one of the fundamental ways to make him your friend is to pray for him. Jesus not only taught this, but practised it. When the final, terrifying process of crucifixion had been accomplished, and the cross had settled shudderingly in its upright position, Jesus prayed: 'Father, forgive them, for they do not know what they are doing.' We know specifically that one of his followers acted precisely in a similar way. As the stones fell relentlessly upon him, crushing his bones and tearing his flesh, Stephen cried: 'Lord, do not remember this sin against them.'

Two categories, however, are beyond our ability to pray for – *the dead* and *the apostate*. The former are beyond the influence of anything which either we or they can do to affect their eternal destiny. The moment we die there is a great unbridgeable gulf fixed and judgement is focused on the things which have been accomplished or otherwise within our earthly span. We may well remember them lovingly and gratefully before God in our prayers of thanksgiving, but to change their eternal course is now beyond us. Prayer by the dead for us and prayer for the dead by us are ruled out by the Bible.

The latter category – the apostate – are impervious to the loving overtures of God's grace to them, and so our prayers for them are irrelevant. They once were open to the Spirit of God, but by one means and another they have resisted God's loving correction, compassion and direction and have turned their backs on the One who gave his life for them. That old, trusted disciple of Jesus, John – the one who loved Jesus so deeply, and whom Jesus so loved and trusted – wrote in one of the most penetrating and demanding letters of the New Testament: 'If you see your brother commit a sin that does not lead to death, you should pray to God who will give him life. This applies to those whose sins do not lead to death. But there is sin which leads to death, and I do not say that you should pray to God about that.' What an awesome warning to the stubborn and the rebellious.'

We need to be clear that this condition is very rare. It will only be found in people who have deliberately, persistently and knowingly resisted God over a long period. We should never make speedy, individual divisions in this area. Such decisions demand spiritual maturity and clear discernment such as are only likely to be found in a group of mature Christians acting in total harmony.

What should we pray for?

Having reached this point we need to ask a further question – what should we pray for when we are praying for others? The directions here are easy to state, but very difficult to be sure of. We are to pray for their **needs** and not their **wants**. It is self-evident that what people need and what they want are two quite different things. These two things are very difficult for us to distinguish in ourselves, and even harder in others.

This familiar dilemma is expressed in the well-known lines:

> *He prayed for strength that he might achieve;*
> *He was made weak that he might obey.*
> *He prayed for health that he might do greater things;*
> *He was given infirmity that he might do better things.*
> *He prayed for riches that he might be happy;*
> *He was given poverty that he might be wise.*
> *He prayed for power that he might have the praise of men;*
> *He was given disappointment that he might feel the*
> *need of God.*
> *He prayed for all things that he might enjoy life;*
> *He was given life that he might enjoy all things.*
> *He had received nothing that he asked for, all that he*
> *hoped for;*
> *His prayer was answered – and he was greatly blessed.*

We urgently need the gifts of knowledge, wisdom and discernment of spirits. Prayer has been greatly impoverished and neutralised because the dimension of the Spirit has been neglected or forbidden. So often our ignorance, our short-sightedness, our humanity and our sentimentality blind us and bewilder us when we pray for others.

This is even more critical when we face the issue of the good – or the best. So often when we are praying for others we sense that the response to our request to God for them would be good – but sometimes there is a lingering doubt: 'Would this be the best for them?' Every parent knows the heart-aching pain of watching his child face up to a set of circumstances which are difficult to handle and even painful to endure – yet the end result of this experience will be a stronger, wiser and more able person. All that is sensitive within us wants to rescue and deliver – but that is not the best way! Happy and blessed is the parent whose wisdom prevails!

Our experience is not different when praying for others – we want, not just the good, but the highest good; the best for them.

How should we pray for others?

This is our final question. How can I make my intercession more effective and real? First of all I need to realise that what God is looking for is quality not quantity. There is something within us which urges us to believe that the longer my prayers are, and the greater number the people who join me in prayer, the more likely I will be to achieve my objective. Jesus, however, is very clear in his directions when he says: 'You will not be heard because of your long prayers' and 'where two or three get together and agree together' God will hear and answer. Jumbo size and record crowds impress us whether referring to an aeroplane or the number on the picket line, but quite obviously both leave God singularly unimpressed in themselves. What God is looking for is depth, reality, honesty and faith in our praying rather than a marathon. His eyes are searching for One Name on the petitions we bring rather than all the others which impress us. Length and numbers have little significance unless these things are present. Assuming these, then, the sacrifice of time and the commitment of many is impressive.

Jesus said to his disciples in the disappointment and despair of their failure to be effective, 'This kind can only be dealt with by prayer and fasting.' In other words 'You missed the cost out of it!' Part of the value of true fasting is that it demonstrates that we are in earnest and we are really committed to what we are doing.

Secondly, we need to be eager to pray for others when they are present with us as well as when they are absent from us. How often we learn of a situation and hear of a need and we then promise: 'I will be remembering you/that in my prayers.' Why not there and then reach out physically and pray for them? It is true that we are not to be too eager to 'lay hands' on people, but we need to recapture the biblical implication of 'the laying on of hands'. It is not merely a symbol, but rather the biblical way for conveying and communicating God's power going into the situation. It has three main contexts.

1. When we are praying for the sick.

2. When we are praying 'in Jesus' name' for a person to be baptised in the Holy Spirit, an experience which should normally be part of our initial conversion. Jesus is the baptiser and we are simply the physical and visible expression of his Body.

3. When we are praying for one of the Lord's servants who is leaving us 'on special mission'.

I have noticed that there is much more instruction in the Bible about the use of our open hands in prayer than there is about our closed eyes.

It hardly seems necessary to mention it again, and yet it brings a completely new dimension into praying for others – God might say to us: 'I want *you* to be part of the *answer* to that prayer that you are now *asking*'. It will not always be so – but it will sometimes – and I think much more often than we might think. God will often use angels and sometimes other human beings to accomplish his purposes – but from time to time he will be looking for *your* availability. Remember, Jesus never did feed the five thousand as he is often credited as doing. 'You yourselves give them something to eat,' he said. 'He ordered the people to sit down on the grass; then he took the five loaves and the two fish, looked up to heaven, and gave thanks to God. He broke the loaves and gave them to the disciples, and the disciples gave them to the people. Everyone ate and had enough' (Matthew 14:19–20). A truly remarkable event, but a clear reminder that God gave the resources and the disciples were the answer to their own concern for a hungry crowd.

Perhaps every prayer for others needs to be concluded with a personal offer: 'If there is some way I can be part of the answer to what I am asking – here I am. I am available. However impossible it may seem to me, and however inappropriate that appears to be, here I am.' This book would never have had my name on it, had it not been for that kind of praying!

In praying for others ask these three questions in the light of what has been said:

1. Who should I now be praying for?

Let God decide. It is so easy to respond emotionally and mentally: 'I will pray for you!' Nothing will more readily cause guilt and a sense of failure than that well-intentioned and yet so often glib remark. We need always to have our eyes on the Lord here – 'Do you want me to be committed to pray for him/her/that, Lord?'

In other words we need to allow the Lord to write our prayer list. Revise the shape of your prayer list regularly before God. Keep it fresh!

2. Is my prayer list too long?

Depth and reality are much more significant than numbers. Precise directions for numbers are difficult to give, but for most of us our prayer list is much too long to be real.

3. Who is the key in this situation, Lord?

We need to ask the Lord for directions here. We need to find the key to unlock the door. You will remember that God loves the world. Jesus, however, did not pray for the world (John 17). He prayed only for eleven men in the world. They were going to prove strategic in the coming of the kingdom of God on earth as it is in heaven. So it has proved to be!

Meditate on: 1 Samuel 12:23; Isaiah 64:7; Ezekiel 22:30,31; 1 Timothy 2:1.

6
The practice of prayer

When I was up at University Dr J. Sidlow Baxter was exercising a powerful and influential ministry in Edinburgh. He once shared the development of his own prayer life. What an encouragement it is when the servants of God allow us the privilege of knowing the deep, intimate and personal stresses in their lives! Dr Baxter decided that the early hour belonged to God, and so he allowed mind to prevail over mattress and got up to give God what belonged to him. When he did this he noticed that his emotions did not go with him to the place of prayer for the first few days. He experienced that dull, heavy, lack-lustre feeling which is often the accompaniment of the first moments after our feet get on the floor in the morning. And so he prayed without emotions, but he continued to get up and meet God in the place of prayer. After several days, one morning he was praying and his emotions decided to join him. That was a good, satisfying time in prayer.

For some years now we have met together as a church at nine o'clock each morning until ten o'clock. It is not the most convenient time for many people to come to pray (although I suspect that it is convenient for more than those who actually do come at that time). We meet in the extension to the old church building and this is a comfortable well-lit place. One particular January morning I was attending that prayer meeting and from the very beginning I sensed a great heaviness. It seemed that there was an air or an atmosphere of dullness over the whole group that had met to pray. In addition, the weather was bleak outside and, unusually, it was cold inside. On that particular morning comparatively few had gathered for prayer. It was a Thursday and normally on that morning we would be concerned to pray for the nation. On that January day talks were going on in Stockholm between the Russian representative Andrei Gromyko and the American representative Mr Schultz about armaments. One of the pastoral team began the time for prayer and, frankly, it lacked inspiration and real conviction. He left the prayer time to its own devices for a bit and then broke in to give some leadership and to encourage praise. This was slow to start, but eventually began to gain spiritual momentum. By the time we separated at ten o'clock there was a real sense of unity and fulfilment amongst us. The time for prayer had become the time for vision and faith. What had begun at a zero-rating, so far as a prayer experience is concerned, had ended on a high note.

If we are ever going to get a realistic hold of prayer we also need to get a hold of the valid principle which these brief testimonies demonstrate. Man, in the area of his soul, has three great capacities. The first is his capacity to **know**, to reason, to think – his **intellectual** capacity. The second is his capacity to **feel** – his **emotional** capacity. The third is his capacity to **decide** – his **will** or **volitional** capacity. This is how we all are and our success in prayer will be determined by the order of authority of these capacities. This is so vitally important!

If our **emotions** reign then our prayer life will suffer greatly. If we wait for the good time; the high moment; the great, surging emotional experience; we will grow discouraged. Our emotions are influenced by so many things which are always changing – our relationships; the accomplishments or frustrations of our job; the amount of sleep we have had; the weather; our digestive system, and so on. Emotions are not wrong, but it is wrong to allow our emotions to rule our lives. The result of allowing our emotions to control us will be continual variations and helpless inconsistencies.

Over the years, I have frequently had the opportunity to prepare people for marriage. I have never found two situations in this kind of preparation which are similar. Each couple brings with them so many different experiences of life, so many influences and attitudes that have helped to shape and fashion them over the years. It is always a great personal delight, but at the same time a very demanding challenge, to be involved in the lives of people at this level. There is one thing, however, among others, which is common and fundamental for every couple. I try to say this in a number of different ways, but all the time my intention is to emphasise this basic ingredient in the relationship of a man and woman in marriage. It is simply that a marriage can never be at the mercy of our feelings. Our feelings fluctuate all the time and if the foundations of marriage are built on how we feel then inevitably the quality of the marriage will constantly be variable. Unhappily many within our society today have allowed their emotional lives to dictate the reality or otherwise of their marriage. The result, of course, is instability, uncertainty and awful vulnerability.

A marriage which is going to be all that God ever intended it to be will be based in the area of the will and on the foundation of commitment. Before a couple marry their relationship depends much more on their feelings for each other than anything else, but after the marriage has taken place their feelings will emerge out of the commitment which they have made to each other and it is on the firm foundation of commitment that future security, fulfilment and joy in marriage will be accomplished. So far as prayer is concerned people have often said to me through the years, 'I do not feel that God is there'. Frankly, I do not know anywhere in the Bible where it

71

says that you should *feel* God is there. We are instructed, however, to 'have faith in God'.

If our **intellect/mind** reigns, the result will be much the same as when our emotions reign. The human mind is at the mercy of its own observations. It has two great weaknesses. It does not have the final report of all the facts on any given subject. Secondly, the facts it does have are coloured by its own interpretations and biased point of view.

Prayer, then, can neither be established nor maintained on emotions or intellect. It is only my **will** which is able to get me into, and then continue in, the adventure of prayer. The **will** is the key. Unlike **emotions**, it has the capacity to act independently of feelings. Unlike the **mind**, it has the capacity to act independently of understanding. The will has the power to do something with which my emotions may not agree nor my mind understand. We must will to pray because the Word of God has both invited and commanded us to pray. I must learn to live then in the area of my will if I am ever to make headway in my praying. The way I feel will continually change, and the way I think will continually persuade me at any given time of a dozen reasons why I should not be praying now. There is no fact that has been more helpful to me over these recent years in every area of living the Jesus life in the power of the Holy Spirit than this one fact.

Determine you will pray, because it is right. Vow to stand with your will in co-operation with the will of God. It is only when I will to be obedient that I can trust the Holy Spirit to come right alongside me to help me in my weakness.

Jesus gives very clear instructions about the features of our prayers. We are to pray with **sincerity**. How easy it is to pray for the things which we ought to pray for rather than the things we either want to pray for or need to pray for. How easy it is to allow the expectations of others, or even the traditional concepts of our own background to dictate the way we pray. Martin Luther's direction is again well remembered, 'The first law of prayer is "don't lie to God!"'

Simplicity is to be another feature of our praying. Jesus taught his disciples a one-minute prayer, and the words that he gave them are the essence of simplicity. One of the great teachers of oriental languages of a past generation, was Dr John Duncan. He was lovingly referred to as 'Rabbi' Duncan. He was on the Faculty of Divinity at Edinburgh University and taught in New College, Edinburgh. His students were so overwhelmed by his knowledge and ability that the story got around that he actually said his prayers in Hebrew. Whether it is apocryphal or not, it is said that two of his students hid outside his room, after he had retired for the night, in order to listen to his praying. They heard the normal noises of the godly old man preparing to go to bed – and then silence. To their astonishment and embarrassment he began to pray aloud:

> *Gentle Jesus, meek and mild,*
> *Look upon a little child.*
> *Pity my simplicity*
> *Suffer me to come to Thee.*

Red-faced humiliation was their experience, but simplicity in prayer was his.

Humility must characterise our praying according to Jesus. Self-righteousness, as well as self-interest, can be the death of prayer. He tells a strong, provocative story of a Jewish leader and a socially-despised tax-collector who went to the temple to pray (Luke 18:9–14). The former congratulated himself before God for his spiritual virtues whilst the latter pleaded nothing other than his need. Comments Jesus, 'I tell you the tax-collector, and not the Pharisee, was in the right with God when he went home.'

Another strong element in our praying is to be **tenacity**. We give up too quickly, and we give in too easily in so many things – but especially in praying. Jesus does not commend long prayers, but he does encourage frequent prayers. 'Pray, and go on praying,' he says. 'Ask, and go on asking. Seek, and go on seeking. Knock, and go on knocking.' We often question

73

why, rather than get on with doing it; we are impoverished as a result. Why are we so reluctant to do what we are told even when the One who is telling us so obviously knows what he is talking about?

Love, too, is to be the climate in which our praying is to be done. The only aspect of the Lord's prayer which Jesus commented on was this one. 'Father, forgive me as I have forgiven him!' This is the only thing I am asked to do. This is the only condition which is inherent in the Lord's Prayer. Get anything which has broken your fellowship with another dealt with – however embarrassing, awkward or inconvenient that may be. It may be that he or she has hurt, misrepresented and wronged you. The situation may be entirely reversed and it is you who have been the offending party (Matthew 5:23,24). Whoever has been responsible, and whatever the circumstances – put it right!

Finally, Jesus assures us, significant things happen through prayer when more than one person is involved in praying for the same thing – so **unity** is another important ingredient in the practice of prayer. Where there is agreement between two or more people on the same issue there is strength and expectation of a positive response from God. Fellowship here, as elsewhere, is so important – it objectifies, corrects, encourages and strengthens. Faith is infectious, and infection spreads where people gather. Unbelief thrives more easily in isolation – and the devil knows it. It was at a united prayer meeting, the climax of several such meetings over a number of days, that the mighty power of Pentecost was unleashed (Acts 2:1,2, see 1:14). It was when the church members 'all joined together in prayer to God' – without criticism or complaint – that 'the place where they were meeting was shaken' and 'they were all filled with the Holy Spirit and began to proclaim God's message with boldness' (Act 4:24–31). The miracle of Peter's release from prison happened when the whole church prayed (Acts 12:5). The great missionary thrust into Asia Minor came when there was a united prayer meeting of church leaders (Acts 13:1–4).

The honest, simple, humble, tenacious, loving praying of the individual is mightily effective, but both Scripture and experience combine to assure us that the agreed, united praying of many is even more so.

Much more important than the **place** of prayer or the **time** of prayer is the **priority** of prayer. Jesus prayed where he could. He did not have a home of his own, far less the privacy of his own bedroom. He used the great outdoors. The climate in which many of us live makes this much more difficult and uncomfortable – but why not wrap up and go for a walk with Jesus? Jesus obviously prayed when confronted with decision-making; when facing crucial moments in his life; when emotion swept over him in a great flood-tide; when life was hectic and the demands overwhelming; when God needed to come through in a miraculous, supernatural way. But he does not seem to have had a specific time-pattern for prayer, as he obviously had for worship. He prayed early in the morning or late at night. He prayed at mid-day or all night. His praying, however, was constantly related to life. If only we could begin to realise that prayer is our first resource rather than our last! Our friendship with God should be a daily and constant thing – and it needs to be expressed.

Bertram Pollock was at one time Bishop of Norwich, and the life of a Bishop must be very busy! In the memoir which she wrote of him, his wife tells how every day in life he had certain times set aside for prayer. No matter who came to see him at these times, he would say, 'Put him in an anteroom and tell him to wait. I have an appointment with God.' We should have these regular appointments with God – to discuss; to talk through; to ask his opinion; to get to know his mind; to begin to understand how he feels about it; to be assured of his encouragement; and so on. That appointment needs to be a priority engagement which nothing should break. There is something shameful in going to a friend only when we need him and when we want to get something out of him; and there is something shameful in treating God as someone to be made use of only when we are in trouble and when life goes wrong. In sunshine and in shadow we should have our times with God. Obviously there will be times when prayer is more intense than at other times; but prayer should be for us a constant thing. 'A man, sir,' said Dr Johnson, 'should keep his friendships in constant repair.'

Over the years my wife and I have returned to the daily readings of Oswald Chambers in *My Utmost for His Highest* to instruct our minds for meditation in the Word of God; to stimulate faith; and to guide us in our praying. In one of these readings there was the memorable caution that 'you can spend half an hour with your habit rather than half an hour with the Lord'. How true! Order, structure and form are only valid so long as they allow life to flow through them. A warm relationship with God who is our Father is what we are looking for rather than a slavish religious ritual which satisfies our ego and little else. For this reason you will find it helpful to notice the following:

1. Change the routine of your praying to meet your need.
2. Be careful about a pattern which has ceased to be viable to bring life and reality through it.
3. Constantly review the Bible-reading notes you are using.
4. Bring your prayer list up to date regularly with sensitivity to what God directs.
5. Be flexible in the time that you set aside for your appointment with God – life and circumstances change so rapidly!
6. Ensure, however, that there is time set aside as there is for eating, travelling to work, dressing etc. The keynote in all of this is that we find time to do the things that we consider to be important.
7. Establish your position as God's child as you come to prayer. Make your own list of Scriptures which will become very personal to you as they affirm who you are in God and what you have become by his grace.

Here is a list which I have written down at the back of my Bible. I have put it there for I constantly need to refer to it. The Bible fortifies us with truth to be used in the battle against the enemy. Since it is truth, it is true all the time, but like a sword in its scabbard, or a gun in its holster, it is useless until gripped firmly in the hand of faith and used in battle. It is the chief work of the devil to isolate me from the continuing consciousness of who I am in Jesus – what God has made me by his grace. If somehow he can get me to the point in my thinking that I am unaware of the reality and the glory of having Christ in me and being, myself, in him, the enemy can so easily accuse, confuse and even defeat me.

So I need to rehearse the truth – to believe and to speak out the Word of God as I prepare to pray. These parts of the Bible refer to my position and my welfare as a child of God in a very personal way. To declare these things openly and regularly in the presence of God, and in the hearing of the hosts of darkness, means that some real praying is about to take place:

I now confess in agreement with God that . . .

I am a forgiven man, and God has brought me out of darkness and put me into the family and kingdom of his dear Son – Colossians 1:13.

With Christ I too have been crucified, so that as I face this day/night it is not any more I who am living, but Christ is living in me. I am living now by faith in the Son of God who loves me, and gave his life for me – Galatians 2:20.

I have received the Spirit because God promised him to me and Jesus came to make that promise real – Galatians 3:14.

My body is the dwelling place of the Holy Spirit, and he is the means by which Christ dwells within me,

enabling me to share in the glory of God –
1 Corinthians 3:16; Colossians 1:27.

I share the glory Jesus experienced from God. My life in this world is the same as Christ's. As he was so am I in the world. I, in all that I am, belong to him; and he, in all that he is, belongs to me – John 17:21–23; 1 Corinthians 3:21–23; 1 John 4:17.

Even before God created the world he wanted me. He has set me free to live a holy life. All of this is on the basis of the undeserved generosity of his heart and not on my ability to do things well – Ephesians 1:4,7,8.

God has given me a rich inheritance because of what Christ has done. As I live in him, and he in me, I can know the reality of God's promises – Galatians 3:15–18.

The resurrection power of God is at work in me. He has raised me to sit with him far above every principality, power, might, and dominion. Nothing under Jesus' feet is over my head, and all things are under his feet – Ephesians 1:19–23.

God has made me what/who I am. In my new relationship with Jesus he has equipped me to do what he always wanted me to do – Ephesians 2:10.

God chose me long before I could respond to him. He set me apart to become like Jesus, and I can have a warm, close relationship with him. He then called me, put me right with himself and shared his glory (i.e. his 'fullness'; his 'brightness') with me. In view of this God is working for good in my life and so I can stand before every circumstance and say, 'If God is for me, who can be against me?' – Romans 8:28–31.

Because of the reality of my relationship with Jesus and my confidence in who he is and what he has done I can go into God's presence with great boldness – Ephesians 3:12.

The glory of God is in marked contrast to me, but he has given me his glory that no one would ever misunderstand that the life and the power that I now display are his and not mine – 2 Corinthians 4:7.

God is supplying all my needs – Philippians 4:19.

I can face anything with the power that Christ keeps on giving me – Philippians 4:13.

God is able to give me more than I need so that I will always have a testimony to his goodness personally and also be able to bless others who are in need – 2 Corinthians 9:8.

I am sure that having begun his good work in me, God will complete it on the Day of Christ Jesus – Philippians 1:6.

I am strong with strength which comes from his glorious power so that I might always be joyful and patient and give thanks to God in all things – Colossians 1:11.

These are only a few verses which affirm our place and standing in God! There are many more! Find them; claim them personally as an act of faith; write them down (what a blessing even writing these things down can be!); if necessary memorise them; above all use them as you come to prayer.

One of the blessings in our worship these days in our church is a song by Keith Green, who was so tragically killed in an air crash with his two children Josiah and Bethany. One of the verses needs to be noted particularly:

I was lied to, but You gave me truth,
   You are the truth;
I was lied to, but You gave the truth to me!

Let us hear the truth; declare the truth; rehearse the truth verbally and audibly. In counselling I have frequently given people their 'prescription' before they leave my office, with the guidance that they are to use it three times a day – in the morning; middle of the day; and in the evening. This prescription is a verse, or usually a few verses from Scripture on a piece of paper. They use it by speaking it out in three directions in turn — to themselves as a reminder of who they are or who God is or what he has done; to the devil as a declaration of fact and faith; and to God as a demonstration of trust and dependence.

As you begin to pray, establish your position as a child in God's family; a citizen in God's kingdom; a servant in the household of faith; and as a soldier in the invincible army of the King.

7
Praying in the name of Jesus

Praying was and is such a vital part of the activity of Jesus. We have sometimes forgotten and often neglected what Jesus is doing *now*! We have so emphasised the divinity of Jesus (and without this conviction one cannot be a Christian) that we have obscured his present humanity. There is a Man in heaven today and, amidst other activity, he is praying for us. Jesus did not simply become human for thirty-three years, but for eternity. Jesus is not only on God's side, he is on our side too. One of the most thrilling disclosures of the Bible is that: '. . . we have a great High Priest who has gone into the very presence of God – Jesus the Son of God. Our High Priest is not one who cannot feel sympathy for our weaknesses. On the contrary, we have a High Priest who was tempted in every way that we are, but did not sin' (Hebrews 4:14–15). Perhaps the reason why this wonderful reality has been obscured is because the Ascension of Jesus is such a neglected doctrine of the Christian faith – although as the Holy Spirit has been poured out upon the people of God one of the immediate effects is to make us aware of who Jesus is and what he is doing now. Many of the contemporary spiritual songs exalt Jesus; declare him to be reigning in majesty and glory; acknowledge his position of authority and power; see him reigning now on high.

The four major Christian festivals from early times were Christmas, Easter, Whitsun and Ascension. For centuries they were held in honour throughout Christendom. Christmas and Easter still keep their supremacy, and with the new awareness among Christians in the West of the person and ministry of God the Holy Spirit, Whitsun too to a lesser degree. But Ascension Day has fallen into neglect. Perhaps the reasons for this are obvious. It is no longer a public holiday. Significantly the House of Commons gives itself a holiday on Derby Day rather than on Ascension Day as it used to. Then, of course, it falls on a Thursday and so does not receive the same emphasis of Sunday preaching and activity as Easter and Whitsun. Perhaps there is an underlying fear, too, that it belongs to a pre-scientific era which believed that the earth is flat and heaven is 'just up there'. My personal conviction is that so important is the spiritual heart and reality of the Ascension that the devil has seen to it by one means or another that we neglect this fundamental reality of Christian belief – Jesus is not dead, he is alive; his work is not ended, it continues; he is not passive, he is active; he is praying – for *me* – *now*!! The Ascension or Exaltation of Jesus is spoken of at least thirty-three times in the New Testament.

S. D. Gordon once wrote:

The Lord Jesus is still praying. Thirty years of living; thirty years of serving; one tremendous act of dying; nineteen hundred years of prayer. What an emphasis on prayer.

Jesus lived praying. He died praying. He continues praying. In one night in history the whole of prayer was changed for us. It was that urgent, emotional night on the eve of his crucifixion when Jesus declared something which was quite new for our prayer life. He said the same thing five times over – use my name in prayer: '. . . I will do whatever you ask for in my name . . .'; 'If you ask for anything in my name, I will do it; '. . . the Father will give you whatever you ask of him in my name'; 'Until now you have not asked for anything in my name; ask and you will receive . . .'.

The name Jesus was given to that tiny baby born in Bethlehem who was God become man, not by his mother or foster-father, but by an angel. The choice of that name caused no anxiety or controversy between the young couple – it was chosen by God! Curiously enough, before he was born, the name Jesus was very popular. Josephus – an historian who lived around the time of Jesus – mentions forty different people called Jesus. Even in the New Testament itself there are five people called Jesus – including Barabbas, who was set free rather than Jesus of Nazareth. Presumably this is why the New Testament refers to him as Jesus of Nazareth – so that he would be distinguished from all the others by the same name. His address is added to ensure his identity.

During his life his name spread out from Galilee – the sick, the disadvantaged, the blind, the critical, the curious, had all heard of him. He was talked about; admired by ordinary people; feared by the authorities – especially those responsible for the dead, hypocritical formalism of religion.

After his death his name was not used. The Jews would no longer use it, because they hated it and would never identify their children by it. The Christians would not use it, because they would have regarded it as blasphemous and irreverent to have called any of their children by that name since it signified the unique, perfect Son of God.

Significantly, when the church began preaching, they did not preach religion or Christianity. Nor did they preach a philosophy or a system of ethics or a code of morality. Surprisingly, they did not speak as often as we might have expected about preaching the gospel – they did speak about preaching Christ. They did not say: 'Join the church!' or 'Accept our philosophy of life!' or 'Try and live like this or like us!' They said 'We want to tell you about a name!' Peter cried to the confused and convicted multitude on that extraordinary day of Pentecost, 'Whoever calls on the name of the Lord will be saved.' Philip, the evangelist, directed by an angel and instructed by the Holy Spirit intruded into the Bible reading of the Chancellor of Ethiopia, as he was travelling in his chariot, and 'told him the good news about Jesus'. An old and unknown disciple of Jesus, Ananias, was persuaded against his will to go and help Saul of Tarsus with these astonishing instructions from the Lord, '. . . I have chosen him to serve me, and make my name known to the Gentiles and kings and to the people of Israel'. Dear, thoughtful John, that specially loved disciple of Jesus categorically states that '. . . as many as received him, to them he gave power to become the sons of God, even to them that believe on his name.'

In other words the distinctive content of the earliest Christian teaching can be summed up in one word – CHRIST! So it always has been where reality and effectiveness have accompanied religion. One of the old church fathers declared, 'Were the highest heavens my pulpit, and the whole host of the redeemed my audience, Jesus alone would be my text.' Martin Luther, too, who set Europe aflame with spiritual revolution exclaimed, 'We preach always Christ, and Christ alone, true God and true man. That may seem a monotonous and limited subject, likely to be soon exhausted, but we are never at the end of it.' That outstanding preacher of a past generation, Alexander Maclaren, claimed as he reviewed the strenuous years of his mighty ministry in Manchester, 'I have tried to preach Jesus Christ, the Jesus Christ, not of the Gospels only, but the Christ of the Gospels and the Epistles.' So preaching is seen to be a supernatural act – the transmission *of* a Person *through* a person *to* a company of persons. The event of preaching is not speaking *about* Jesus, but communicating him to others in the power of the Holy Spirit.

As a result of this **forgiveness** becomes a possibility through the name of Jesus (Luke 24:45–49). The answer of our society to a guilty conscience is forget your sins; or excuse your sins since you are human and fallible like everyone else; or blame your sins on others and let them carry the responsibility. But Jesus says clearly that we can call on his name and be clean. In fact we will never know the reality of forgiveness of sins, and the freedom of a clear conscience, unless and until we hear the name Jesus. There is no help or hope anywhere else.

Not only does the name of Jesus make forgiveness possible, but it makes **fellowship** actual. His name validates pardon and joins people together. He accomplishes, not simply an agreement of minds or a sharing of interests, but a real life commitment. Fellowship is one of the most severely debased words in our language, both inside and outside the church. Paul, writing with an aching heart to the divided fellowship of God's people in Corinth, says: 'Now, I appeal to you, my brothers, by the Name of our Lord Jesus Christ that you all agree in what you say, so that there will be no divisions among you. Be completely united, with only one thought and one purpose.' This must for ever remain a pipe-dream, an unattainable ideal apart from the name of Jesus. A denominational loyalty will never achieve it, nor will theological agreement – only Jesus will. What we have spoken of as fellowship so often has only been natural kinship, but what the Bible speaks of as fellowship is humanly speaking absurd and impossible – it is a superhuman and supernatural reality, made possible through the name of Jesus.

Christian **service** is also affected by the name of Jesus. After many years as a pastor, I am bound to say that most problems in Christian service arise from the fact that we do it for the wrong person or the wrong people. We do what we do so often for the church or the organisation (especially a para-church organisation!), for the denomination of which we are a part, or even for ourselves. When things are difficult and, in our view, success has eluded us, and people have become critical of us we so easily become disillusioned and resentful of the people who are part of these things. So it is that Paul categorically points out that 'everything you do or say, then, should be done in the name of the Lord Jesus'. This is the difference between our *old* life and our *new* life. It answers the question: 'Who are you doing this for anyway?' I remember sharing in a baptismal service one Sunday evening in our church. It was one of those joyous, memorable events when certain things remain clearly in your memory. One of the men baptised that night was wearing a white tee-shirt across the front of which in bold black lettering were the simple words: 'Under New Management'. Wouldn't it be a radical step for all of us if everything we did from now onwards was done in the name of Jesus? Wouldn't it create a whole new dimension of reality if we married in the name of Jesus; if we cared for, supported and nourished our family in the name of Jesus; if we earned our living, not because of the National Health Service or the Education Authority or London Transport or the Trade Union Congress or the Confederation of British Industry or whoever it is, or whatever it is, we work for, but because of Jesus; if we took our responsibility within our local church in the name of Jesus?

Ministry, too, becomes not only real, but powerful when it is done in the name of Jesus. There is power over every enemy of man in the name of Jesus. The Bible very clearly teaches the relevance of the name of Jesus when we are dealing with both the demonic and the diseased. The astonished disciples returned to Jesus on one occasion with a remarkable testimony: 'Lord', they said, 'even the demons obeyed us when we gave them a command in your name.' There is no longer any need for fear or the re-telling of horror stories when we are confronting the powers of darkness – the name of Jesus is sufficient and devastatingly effective.

> *Jesus! the name high over all,*
> *In hell, or earth, or sky;*
> *Angels and men before it fall,*
> *And devils fear and fly.* (Charles Wesley)

The startled beggar at the door of the Temple could never have imagined the power of the name of Jesus before Peter said to him, 'I have no money at all, but I give you what I have; in the name of Jesus Christ of Nazareth I order you to get up and walk.' I hesitate to record these things in this book, for I frequently wonder what has changed! Where is this power in this country today? I know that in many parts of the world such power is being clearly demonstrated. Where is it among us and within me, authenticating the gospel which I preach and bringing glory and honour to the God whom I serve? Its absence in so much of our ministry today, however, does not invalidate its reality, but acts simply as an uncomfortable spur to compel us to ask questions in order that we would get answers.

Suffering becomes an accompaniment of the name of Jesus. So long as we preach social consciousness or political involvement or moral and ethical responsibility there are not too many problems. But as soon as we declare the name of Jesus there is trouble. The history book of the New Testament (the Acts of the Apostles) gives clear evidence of this. Jesus never gave any grounds that it would be otherwise. It is a proven historical fact that people generally hate the name of Jesus. Hence Jesus' warning shortly before he left his disciples: 'Before all these things take place, however, you will be arrested and persecuted; you will be handed over to be tried in synagogues and be put in prison; you will be brought before kings and rulers for my name's sake' (Luke 21:12). Such a reaction from the human heart is only supportable when we are fully convinced and prepared for it as we reckon on the response to the name of Jesus. We should be clear that we are not suffering for anything else (e.g. our own stupidity or stubbornness or selfishness), but we will suffer for the name of Jesus.

It is into this rich context and remarkable dimension that we insert **prayer** in the name of Jesus. In fact you will never learn the secret of answered prayer until you learn what it means to pray in the name of Jesus. Many people pray – in fact at some time most people pray. I was speaking only last evening to a young woman who claimed that she had been an atheist. Then she was diagnosed to have cancer – and was feeling both physically and emotionally destroyed. As she lay on her bed one afternoon in this shattered condition, she told me that for the first time in her conscious memory she prayed. Prayer doesn't make a person Christian – although God does love to hear the deep cry of the human heart however ignorant of him and ill-informed about spiritual reality it might be. In her case this was so, and I was speaking to her on the eve of her baptism in the name of Christ.

Jesus made some earth-shattering and mind-blowing statements about praying in his name. He used phrases like 'whatever you ask for' and 'if you ask for anything'. Can we dare to believe that Jesus was really speaking the truth when he said that and that he meant what he said? If he was, and if he did, it would really transform our praying out of a deadly dull spiritual chore into a thrilling, enthralling, eagerly anticipated experience.

You may well ask: 'Does that mean that if I asked for a million pounds in his name I would get them?' My answer would be quite simply: 'No, but I will tell you of someone who did ask for a million pounds in his name, and he got them.' There is another question to be asked, you see. We need to ask: 'Why do I want a million pounds?' The person of whom I am speaking was George Müller of Bristol. He asked God to supply his need because he wanted the world to know not only that God could and would do a thing like that, but also because there were little orphaned, disadvantaged children to be cared for – and that was what the money was needed for – and God loves children!

Perhaps I can best illustrate the significance of praying in the name of Jesus by drawing your attention to two very common usages of a name. A *cheque* is useless if it does not have a name on it. The date can be there; the beneficiary's name can be clearly stated; the amount payable to him can be clearly indicated in letters and figures; yet without a name at the bottom as the signatory the cheque is a worthless piece of paper. The value of that cheque depends on the credit behind that name. If I am overdrawn on my current account and my Bank Manager has alerted me to that fact, then I may write out a cheque for you, but it is worthless because there is no credit behind the name. So it is in the Bank of Heaven – only Jesus' name has credit there – no other has!! We are overdrawn on the Bank of Heaven. No matter how good or godly we are we have all drawn more on God than he has ever received from us. Our name, then, on a prayer will not be acceptable. But Jesus' credit is good. On that last night before his crucifixion Jesus was urging his disciples to draw on his name, because his credit is good. 'Use my name,' he says, 'and that will overcome your poverty and destitution.'

To use the name of Jesus in prayer is so much more than appending a little phrase at the end of a prayer. It is realising my poverty and his riches. I have a letter rack on my desk that was given to me one night at a dinner in the United States. The side of the rack which faces me every day in the office says: 'This certifies that the supply of all your need has been deposited in the Treasury of Heaven.' The leaves of the letter rack are in the shape and design of a dollar bill and at the bottom of that same leaf which faces me is the bold statement 'payable on request'. On the side of the letter rack which faces out to anyone who comes to see me in my office is the text of Philippians 4:19, 'And with all his abundant wealth through Christ Jesus, my God will supply all your needs.'

Does this mean that Jesus has given me in prayer then a book of blank cheques for the Bank of Heaven to be used according to my latest whim or fancy? No, it does not mean that at all. Alongside the use of a name in signing a cheque there needs to be taken another way in which we quite commonly use a name. That is to be prepared to sign a *petition*. Jesus doesn't give his name to every blank cheque – we need to ask him: 'Will you put your name on my petition?' To pray in Jesus' name is to bring a petition and say to him: 'Will you sign this, please?' So it needs to be something to which he will gladly sign his name. There are some petitions which Jesus will never sign. You may remember that two of his inner circle of disciples – James and John – asked him to ensure that they would be number two and number three in his kingdom. Jesus refused to put his name on that petition. When Jesus said: 'Use my name in prayer' he was saying: 'Get my name on your petition, and you will get what you are asking for'. The one name that God is looking for on any petition of ours is the name of his own dear Son.

These are two very practical guidelines to the thrilling potential of praying 'in the name of Jesus'. To realise this and respond to it is to enter a new concept of praying. Attached to these five little words is one of the most remarkable promises of Scripture, the promise of *unlimited answer to prayer*. The problem is, of course, that many of us have prayed, using this phrase, and yet our prayers have gone unanswered. Honesty and the demand to know reality make us ask: Why? The reason normally is that we have an inadequate understanding, not only of what the phrase means, but of what it involves. Even more personally, *what it involves us in*.

The great confusion arises because we have laid the emphasis on the idea that primarily prayer is a means of meeting *our* needs. In fact prayer, and especially prayer 'in the name of Jesus' is primarily a means of fulfilling the *purposes of God*. This is why the pattern prayer which Jesus gave his disciples (often referred to as the Lord's Prayer) begins with petitions for *God's* name to be hallowed; for *his* kingdom to come; and for *his* will to be done on earth as it is done in heaven.

One of the Lord's servants testifies that he experienced a breakthrough in intercessory prayer when he began to pray with a view to what God wanted in every situation about which he was praying. He had been in the habit of praying: 'Lord, please help that person (for whom I have a concern). Lord, please attend to this need (that I feel). Lord, come here; Lord, go there.' He changed his whole approach, and began to pray something like this: 'Lord, what can I do to help *you* with *your* plan – for this person; for this need; for that situation?' The change was almost immediate. He was praying with new authority and power. He was no longer representing his own interests to God – he was presenting Jesus' interests to God. He was Jesus' personal representative, and so Jesus' purposes and programme were his now. If we really want to enter this amazing dimension of praying 'in the name of Jesus' we need to begin to become aware of the desires of the heart of Jesus, and present them to God.

1. Have I really considered how much power there is in the name of Jesus?
2. Could Jesus really put his name to what I am asking God for?
3. Are my prayer requests really what the heart of God desires for the fulfilling of his purposes and the completing of his programme?

Epilogue

I have become aware over the years that two areas are uniquely used to cause a sense of guilt and frustration and disappointment among Christians both young and old – the poverty of our prayer life and the faithlessness and disobedience that we show in the handling of our money. As a pastor I have become hesitant in dealing with both. In western society in particular we have become consumed by activism on the one hand and so have lost the prayerful meditation of our eastern brethren, and conditioned by materialism on the other hand and so have avoided the clear instructions of the Bible with regard to handling our possessions. Only the gracious, but persuasive, insistence of the Managing Editor of Scripture Union enabled me to write as I have done. I am no expert when it comes to praying – it is easier to write about it than to do it! Those who know me best are aware of my weaknesses most. I need you to know that I have been challenged again and, in a measure, changed by my own writing. I am not leading you so much as joining you as we get into learning to pray together. I could not know all who will read what I have written, but in anonymity I am praying for you – and perhaps you would pray for me.

In prayer we are in conflict with our natural self – the natural self recoils from God and our fallen nature wants to hide as ever from the presence of God. When it comes to prayer we are all children – vulnerable and impressionable – learning from our heavenly Father.

Prayer is such a paradox – it is so straightforwardly simple and yet so demandingly complex. It describes the most disarmingly simple speech from infant lips and yet embodies the sublime strains of the most devoted disciple reaching the majesty on high. It is appropriate to both the honourable questionings of the aged philosopher and delighted self-consciousness of the little child. It is the urgent, concise expression of the moment and yet is the attitude of a life-time. It contains the deep, yearning agony of the dark valley, but also the winged, liberated ecstasy of the mountain top. It can with certainty lay hold on God and at the same time with authority immobilise the devil. It can pin-point with remarkable relevance a single precise and even trivial personal objective and yet roam the world with intrusion into national and international affairs. It can contain heart-broken, abject confession and also rapt and splendid adoration. It invests puny man with a sort of omnipotence so that properly understood he will pay lip-service to its value and potency and yet so often he will fail to pray. Such is the reality that we are involved in together. For expert guidance and inspiration look elsewhere than this book – look at God's book. There you will find the realities of the servants of God. There you will meet a Daniel, who for over seventy years and through five reigns as Prime Minister of mighty Babylon, wielded a prodigious influence – resulting in the breaking of the chains of Babylonian captivity and the glorious setting free of God's people to fulfil God's purposes. You will find that literally no one could keep him on his feet when the appointed hour for prayer arrived. He was opposed by visible enemies and invisible adversaries. He learned that it was invisible forces which ruled the world, and that the course of global events can be influenced by the persistent praying of one man.

Among God's servants you will find logic in prayer; steadfastness in prayer; conflict in prayer; faith in prayer; ambition in prayer; simplicity in prayer; wrestling in prayer; prayers which are wordless; prayers which are eloquent; prayers which are lonely; prayers which are united; prayers which are bold; prayers which are hesitant; prayers which falter; prayers which are unceasing. But you will also find the prayers, not only of God's servants, but also of God's Son.

With wonder, watch and listen – and then ask: 'Lord, teach me to pray like that – please!'